cringe

Sarah Brown is the host and creator of the Cringe reading series, which began in Brooklyn, New York, in 2005. Her writing has appeared online at *McSweeney's, Gawker, The Morning News,* and her personal website, www.queserasera.org. She's been published previously in *Created in Darkness by Troubled Americans: The Best of McSweeney's Humor Category* and *Things I Learned About My Dad: Humorous and Heartfelt Essays.* This is her second book.

edited by
SARAH BROWN

Michael O'Mara Books Limited

First published in Great Britain in 2009 by
Michael O'Mara Books Limited
9 Lion Yard
Tremadoc Road
London SW4 7NQ

A CIP catalogue record for this book is available from the British Library.

Papers used by Michael O'Mara Books Limited are natural, recyclable products
made from wood grown in sustainable forests. The manufacturing processes
conform to the environmental regulations of the country of origin.

ISBN: 978-1-84317-345-8

1 2 3 4 5 6 7 8 9 10

www.mombooks.com

Photograph of Doogie Howser on p59 © Twentieth Century Fox/Everett/Rex

Cover design by Ana Bjezancevic

Designed and typeset by Burville-Riley Partnership

Printed and bound in Great Britain by Clays Ltd, St Ives plc

For Nick

KEEP OVT!

CONTENTS

PARENTS

LOVE & SEX

SELF-EXPRESSION

ALCOHOL & DRUGS

FRIENDS & ENEMIES

ACKNOWLEDGEMENTS

There are many people without whom this book would not exist. I'd like to thank: Lindsay Davies, Kerry Chapple, Ana Sampson and everyone at Michael O'Mara Books; Jim Fitzgerald, Anne Garrett and Kate Walker for their advice and guidance; The Foundry in Shoreditch, and both Bardens Boudoir and The Lion in Stoke Newington for hosting London Cringe; O'Neills Bar on Suffolk Street for hosting Dublin Cringe; Jay Carlson and Aaron Dallas for the website building and help; Tiffany Broyles, Antonia Cornwell and Sarah Franklin for all their assistance with setting up Cringe from across an ocean; Nick Hughes and my family for all their support and encouragement; Antonia Cornwell, again, for everything; and most importantly, all the former teenagers and hilariously good sports who've read at London or Dublin Cringe and contributed to this book.

INTRODUCTION

I began hosting Cringe as a monthly reading series at Freddy's Bar in Brooklyn, New York in April 2005. Brave souls would come forward and read aloud from their teenage diaries, journals, notes, letters, poems, abandoned rock operas and other general representations of the crushing misery of their humiliating adolescence. It was (and is) cheaper and better than therapy.

Cringe first came to London in June 2007, in the basement of The Foundry in Shoreditch. Everyone asked, 'Do you think this sort of humour will transfer well? Aren't the British more reserved?' (I'm all for these kinds of broad national stereotypes, as you can tell by how often I shoot my Stars and Stripes pistols into the air and shout, 'Yee-ha!') I had faith that the fact that everyone was once a miserable teenager would be a concept that would cross all cultural barriers, and I was right: the London Cringes have been some of the funniest on record, and the Dublin Cringe in October 2008 was right up there with the best. No matter the country or culture, there are always people with enough bravery and a wrong enough sense of humour to stand up in front of a few friends and a lot of strangers and poke fun at their dramatic former selves. These are my people.

Spin magazine has called Cringe 'the funniest night out in New York,' and the *London Paper* gave it four stars. It's been featured in all forms of media all over the world, from television to radio to print. It was on the front page of the *Los Angeles Times* and featured on an hour-long segment on an Australian radio station. This sort of shared pain and humour has the power to cross lines and unite former angry goths from all over the globe.

I always tell people who are unsure what to read at Cringe to pick the excerpt that physically makes them cringe when they read it to themselves, the one that makes you think, 'I can't read *that* part.' But then when you do, and the room erupts in laughter and everyone groans, you suddenly think, 'Oh, I can top that.' You are among friends. We were all the same teenager underneath. And aren't you glad you never have to be that person again?

Sarah Brown
July 2009

Editor's note:

The following diary extracts have only been very lightly edited and so many of the original spelling and punctuation mistakes remain in all their glory, though some names have been changed in order to protect the innocent (or guilty). All the original extracts have been set in italics, while the adult commentaries are in roman type.

Most of the entries are British, though there are a few contributions from our Australian and American cousins, many of whom now live in the UK. It's interesting to note how their entries reflect the universal nature of teenage angst, though at least these contributors were spared the misery of spending most of their teenage years hanging out in front of Greggs on a drizzly Sunday afternoon.

ANGST

You are no longer a child, and not yet an adult. Everything is horrible and nothing is fair and you're not in charge of anything, least of all your hormones.

The most popular answer is typically death, but there would be fewer entertaining diaries that way.

CRUELEST TRAGEDY

ANN BAYLIS

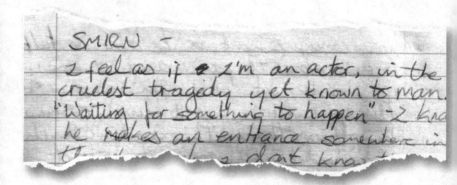

SMIRN –
I feel as if I'm an actor, in the cruelest tragedy yet known to man.
'Waiting for something to happen' – I know he makes an entrance
somewhere in the play, only I don't know the script, or the scene.
I did something very strange the other day. I went through my old
diary, ripping out entries. Some of them were boring, some
embarrassing, some of them I had just made up out of wishful
thinking when I was bored. And you know why I ripped them out?
Because I thought that at some point in my life, I'll be close enough to
him to show him the diary – and I wouldn't have wanted him to read
that sort of thing.

It's so strange – when – and not if – he comes into my life – I
want to be honest with him – I want to tell him that for many years
(well, OK, it's over 1 at the moment) I felt this way towards him –
even though I don't know him at all right now.

Evila

My best friend and I, during the peak years of teenage angst, kept a series of 'letter books' to one another. We would pour out our respective teenage torment onto the pages every night, and exchange books the next morning in school. This proved an unsurprisingly effective method of eliciting some very choice tripe indeed.

This one was written around 1990, so I would have been fifteen or so. What amuses me about this page in particular is reading that, at age fifteen, I had been busily editing my old diary (pifflingly puerile output of a mere fourteen-year-old, no doubt) in order to guard against future embarrassment.

Incidentally, I regret to tell you that SMIRN is short for 'Smirnoff'. I would be morally obliged to savagely rip the piss out of my dear friend's fabulously cheesy choice of nickname, were it not for the fact that I appeared to sign myself off as 'Evila' . . .

JESUS

ALEX FRITH

edge it needs;

Briefly today: flicking cards into a box + talking
for far too long on the phone. And a perfunctory bit of work
(actually. I don't really know what that means, but I
think 'little' comes into the definition somewhere — How

Wednesday 27 March: B (–)

I just saw myself in the mirror & thought I looked like Jesus. That's just
going too far. It's this loose sweatshirt I'm wearing. Too white +
comfortable + of course my rather dismal chin hair. I really should get
around to that Passion picture[1]. Is a smile really all the edge it needs?

Briefly today: flicking cards into a box + talking for far too long
on the phone. And a perfunctory bit of work (actually I don't really
know what that means, but I think 'little' comes into the definition
somewhere) – How is it possible to know the idea of a word but not its
exact meaning? A weird noise heard in probably a single context. But
that's normal for most cultures today, I guess.

One of the best episodes yet of Friends; ER also worth yesterday's
wait. England won 1–0 (vs Bulg), but I haven't yet seen the goal.

This entry was definitely written in the Easter holidays, so I had
probably just been on a school Christian group camp and thoughts
of Jesus were not far from me . . . One of the principles of the sort
of Christianity I was taught is to see Jesus in everyone, which in
theory should help you be nicer to people and less judgmental.
Or, it makes you look in the mirror and get a little God-headed.

[1] A picture of Jesus on the cross.

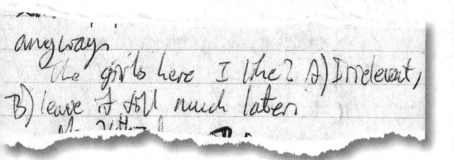

anyway
the girls here I like? A) Irrelevant,
B) leave it till much later

Sunday 23 July: C+ (+)

Don't know. The old 'not fitting in' feeling still there, but I'm really starting to think this is a normal + probably safer attitude to have. Does anyone really 'fit-in' anywhere? There are super-adaptoids[2] like JW, but that's v. different.

I am hoping that maybe working with 5-year-olds will reawaken my sense of fun. Be about damn time, anyway.

The girls here I like? A) Irrelevant, B) leave it till much later.

In July 2004 I had turned sixteen, completed my GCSEs and was in the middle of a very long summer holiday. To fill that time, I'd joined a volunteer group to help run a children's play scheme for a week in sunny Portsmouth. Anyway, I knew a few of the people in the group (such as my super-adaptoid friend JW), but most were a lot older than me and I was obsessed with the idea that I wasn't cool enough to be of any interest to them, in particular the girls. Although clearly I still thought I might have a shot at that later.

---

[2] 'Super-adaptoid' is a reference to an obscure Marvel Comics robot who could adapt to cope with any situation.

EVEN THE HORSES ARE MY ENEMIES

NINA GOTUA

This diary entry was written a week into teenhood, from a summer camp in France. My family considered stays there to be improving to the mind and French fluency, and I considered them exile. My angsty introspection starts with a meditation on a rabbit that my room-mates (Masha and Carolina) and I had found and hidden in a cardboard box for a few days before setting it loose. Here are all the cringe-worthiest aspects of my teenage experience: loss, betrayal, feelings of friendless abandonment, soul-crushing angst, bad songs about loneliness, wrath and the Machiavellian nature of teenage friendships. I wish I could put 'I have retreated to my world of shadows' as my Out of Office message.

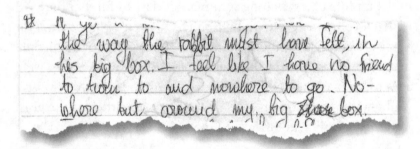

Friday 30 July 1993
Now I feel the way the rabbit must have felt, in his big box. I feel like I have no friend to turn to and nowhere to go. Nowhere but around my big box. I feel like everybody has left me, even hope. Masha finds me dull, she is turning to Carolina. Never had shadows of despair loomed over me so big, not even the day my father died. No, not even then, for

a warm glow of my grandma's love, shone bright in my prison cell of shadows. But now I have no one. No one to turn to, and I too have feelings. Last night I cried. Really cried. But even then I didn't dare cry loud. Only stifled sobs shook my shoulders while my tears dropped on the pillow besides me. Masha does not like me anymore. It is easy for her since she has so many others. Even when she comes back to London she will have great things to do. But for me there is nothing but shadows. Yes, only shadows and my world coloured grey. Yesterday, I made up a song. It goes like this:

> AND WHAT SHOULD I SHOW,
> FOR I HAVE NO FRIEND.
> No FRIEND.
> I'M LOST IN MY WORLD OF GREY.

What should I do,
Where should I go,
What should I see,
And what should I show,
For I have no friend.
No friend.
I'm lost in my world of grey.
What should I do,
Where should I go,
I wish this night would end.[1]

The song of my feelings. For I have no friend. Only you. Yes, only you. Sometimes I feel just like a decoration. Foolish, useless decoration, to sit and watch and admire. Yes and pretend to be cheerful. Well, how can I be cheerful? How? Yes, how can I be nice when my world is falling around me like the walls of Jericho?

---

[1]Roughly to the tune of 'Part of Your World' from *The Little Mermaid* soundtrack. It goes on in this vein for far too many stanzas.

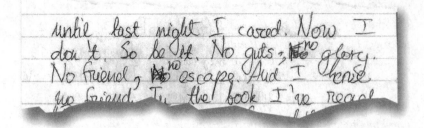

Until last night I cared. Now I don't. So be it. No guts, no glory. No friend, no escape. And I have no friend. In the book I've read 'Flowers in the Attick' four children are locked up, hidden in a room and the attick. They longed for the Sun and the outdoors while I long for friends and hope. In a way we're both flowers stranded in the big shadowy attick.

Today even the horses seemed to really want to be my ennemies. I had this stupid horse called Vermont. He never obeyed. And then he did gallop. Of course I lost my balance immediately. I got hold of his neck but soon enough I was on the ground. Only one of my feet was still in the stirrup and the horse kept on running with me dragging behind him like a flag. After somehow the horse was stopped and my foot freed, I could breathe normal again. But then Vermont stepped on my foot. I felt like breaking his stupid head, but I managed to control myself. Still, horseriding cheered me up. I guess I am unfair to Masha, but anyway she has been neglecting me and after all I'm sick and tired of making excuses for everybody including the horses. We have to put on a play tonight and people don't even know their scripts! I really can't figure Masha out. Sometimes she seems so nice other times she is a bitch, at least for my taste. Carolina is the same except she is bitchy more often. Now my knee is really beginning to hurt me, I knew I had damaged something! Well, I've decided this. Carolina is a bitch! She is. I mean her sister came and told me her friend had sent her a letter and so Carolina rushed off to tell Masha all about it, while she ignored me. Great! I got to know about this because I asked her sister. Now that is unfair. Real unfair! But then again I had expected it. It is obvious that

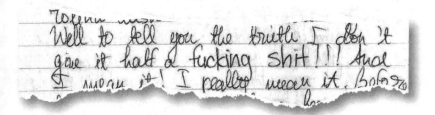

Carolina doesn't like me, not anymore. Well to tell you the truth I don't give it half a fucking shit!!! And I mean it! I really mean it. Before last night I would have been really badly hurt but today, I am not. Don't ask me why it's just that way. Well at least I'm glad I know it now. One bitch of the worst kind is off my neck. And I am happy about it. I am really.

In about two hours we will have that fucking play. Sorry about the vocabulary, these days I don't choose. I don't know if I should tell Masha I don't like Carolina, I mean she will probably just get angry. You can never know. Soon I'll go retreat to my world of shadows.

SOLUTION =
SUICIDE

ALICE GREEN

REASONS I HATE MY LIFE (11 June 1990)
School – Mrs Millner + my jewelry
– Carol McClusky + fighting
– No proper friends except Lee-Anne
– Work is difficult + boring

11 June 1990

REASONS I HATE MY LIFE

School   – Mrs Millner + my jewelry
           – Carol McClusky + fighting
           – No proper friends except Lee-Anne
           – Work is difficult + boring

Home   – Not allowed to use phone for 1 week
           – Parents virtually chain me to my room
           – Keep having massive arguments
           – Everyone picks on me all the time
           – No freedom
           – No harmony
           – Everyone hates everyone else (bad undercurrents)
           – Not allowed to stay out late
           – Not allowed to use phone after 9.30pm

Work   – Tiring and boring
           – Keep getting in trouble

– Badly paid

Friends – Paranoid about Tom
– In love with Barry (huge mistake)
– Not allowed to see Andy hardly ever
– Vast numbers of people don't like me
– Haven't seen anyone but Tom + Lee-Anne for weeks
– Louise has moved to Australia leaving me best-friend-less

Church – Don't want to get confirmed
– Don't like people much anymore
– Don't ENJOY going at all now

Other – Work experience is such a pain
– Parents are so unreasonable
– Life is disorganized
– I'm far too immature
– I'm too fat!
– Keep being called a goth
– Never got any money
– Tired all the time
– Bunk a lot now
– Smoke quite a lot
– Started drinking regularly
– Keep on crying all the time

SOLUTION = Commit suicide

Oh, the melodrama! Carol McClusky was a nasty spiteful girl who wanted to fight me because she knew I would lose. Mrs Millner was a teacher who wanted me to abide by the school uniform policy, which I obviously thought was totally unreasonable. I'm amused that I was obviously so keen to find things to add to my list that I mentioned my parents' unreasonable phone policy twice.

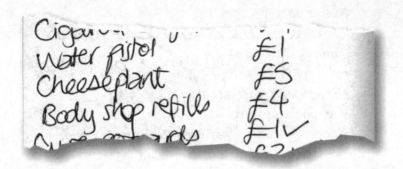

Finances

Alex's 3 Cure posters	£10
Ring for Lee	£10
B'day candles	50p
Thomas plastic watch	£5
Embroidery silks	£2
Blank tapes	£3
Cigarette lighter	£1
Water pistol	£1
Cheeseplant	£5
Body Shop refills	£4
Cure postcards	£1
Powder	£2
Money at present	0p
	(aargh!!)

This entry made me laugh because it obviously seemed incredibly serious at the time that I couldn't afford blank tapes and a cheeseplant. The embroidery silks were to make friendship bracelets out of – clearly that was a priority. Considering I was fifteen at the time of writing, I'm guessing I also wished to purchase my first cigarette lighter for the purposes of smoking illicit Consulate by the school gates.

AND REPEAT

BRITT LINDSAY

> 10. Giving up sweets ... ... will make me a better ...
> 11. Giving up sweets and cigarettes will make me a better person.
> 12. Giving up sweets and cigarettes will make me a better person
> 13. Giving up will not clean my flat, fix my relationship, help me get good marks or make my shitty job less shit but it will make me a better person.
> 14. Giving up sweets and cigarettes will make me a better person.
> 15. Giving up sweets and cigarettes will make me a better person.
> 16. Giving up sweets and cigarettes will make me a better person.
> 17. Giv... ...rette... will make me a ...

24 February 1996

1.   *Giving up sweets and cigarettes will make me a better person.*
2.   *Giving up sweets and cigarettes will make me a better person.*
3.   *Giving up sweets and cigarettes will make me a better person.*
4.   *Giving up sweets and cigarettes will make me a better person.*
5.   *Giving up sweets and cigarettes will make me a better person.*
6.   *Giving up sweets and cigarettes will make me a better person.*
7.   *Giving up sweets and cigarettes will make me a better person.*
8.   *Giving up sweets and cigarettes will make me a better person.*
9.   *Giving up sweets and cigarettes will make me a better person.*
10. *Giving up sweets and cigarettes will make me a better person.*
11. *Giving up sweets and cigarettes will make me a better person.*
12. *Giving up sweets and cigarettes will make me a better person.*
13. *Giving up will not clean my flat, fix my relationship, help me get good marks, make me pretty or make my shitty job less shit but it will make me a better person.*
14. *Giving up sweets and cigarettes will make me a better person.*
15. *Giving up sweets and cigarettes will make me a better person.*

16. *Giving up sweets and cigarettes will make me a better person.*
17. *Giving up sweets and cigarettes will make me a better person.*
18. *Giving up sweets and cigarettes will make me a better person.*
19. *Giving up sweets and cigarettes will make me a better person.*
20. *Giving up sweets and cigarettes will make me a better person.*
21. *Giving up sweets and cigarettes will make me a better person.*
22. *Giving up sweets and cigarettes will make me a better person.*
23. *Giving up sweets and cigarettes will make me a better person.*
24. *Giving up sweets and cigarettes will make me a better person.*
25. *Giving up sweets and cigarettes will make me a better person.*
26. *Giving up sweets and cigarettes will make me a better person.*
27. *Giving up sweets and cigarettes will make me a better person.*
28. *Giving up sweets and cigarettes will make me a better person.*
29. *Giving up sweets and cigarettes will make me a better person.*
30. *Giving up sweets and cigarettes will make me a better person.*
31. *Giving up sweets and cigarettes will make me a better person.*
32. *Giving up sweets and cigarettes will make me a better person.*
33. *Giving up sweets and cigarettes will make me a better person.*

My major flaws:
1. Obsessed with/easily distracted by television
2. Don't keep a clean house
3. Obsessed (negatively) with body image.
4. Rationalise everything/don't accept responsibility for my actions

My major flaws:
1. *Obsessed with/easily distracted by television*
2. *Don't keep a clean house*
3. *Obsessed (negatively) with body image*
4. *Rationalise everything/don't accept responsibility for my actions*

What's most embarrassing about this is that I was obviously trying to be some kind of amateur life-coach by writing such affirming sentences over and over. And, as much as I hate to admit it, I think my major flaws are still the same. I still eat sweets and smoke cigarettes, but I'd like to think I'm a better person now than I was when I was a boyfriend-cheating, basement studio flat-living, pizza-delivering, academic probation-failing nineteen-year-old.

DEAR SOMEBODY

ANTONIA CORNWELL

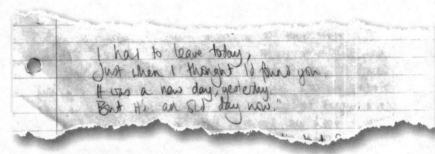

Listen to this. It's a DH Lawrence quote:-

> 'Love – love – love – what does it all mean? What does it
> amount to? So much personal gratification. It doesn't lead
> anywhere.'

How pessimistic! It's so sad when people think like that. It's from The
Rainbow – the bit that ends the novel, I've just been told. Dear oh dear.

> 'Oh, I want to see you soon,
> But I wonder how?
> It was a new day yesterday,
> But it's an old day now.
>
> I had to leave today,
> Just when I thought I'd found you
> It was a new day yesterday
> But it's an old day now.'

– No, not me being poetic, but 2 choruses of a Jethro Tull song I happen to be listening to – and how accurate they are! To think last night we were cuddling in front of the telly – <u>such</u> a warm summer night – he looked so gorgeous, felt so good to hold, was so nice and relaxed – and now he's about 40 fucking miles away. And of course there had to be a feature about Brighton on Blue Peter today.

This just makes me laugh. Clearly I rated Jethro Tull above D. H. Lawrence.

21 March 1988

I would be extremely happy if it weren't for the troubles on my mind. London Transport have found me out, fare-dodging and I'm waiting for the letter through the door that'll tell me what's going to happen to me. They'll never let me go just like that. I always seem to be getting into scrapes, each one more serious than the last, and how I wish I hadn't got into this one. Life would be absolute – well almost perfection if I wasn't in trouble. Why almost perfection? Well that French twit's still staying with us and although tonight's his last night here, it seems like tomorrow will never come and get rid of him.

I'm so nervous about the Letter. The postman's bike was never such an ominous sight as this morning, something seemed to say he knows, he's against you, he'll post that Letter after you've gone and your mother will read it. I do hope the Letter didn't arrive this morning.

I shall tell you a Secret. If the Letter means a lot of Trouble do you know what I'm going to do? I am going to Commit Suicide, which nobody knows but me, and this time I am serious because it is such a Secret.[1]

I will have to do it, which unfortunately will upset everyone – but much as I hate to see loved ones upset, they would have hated me more for being a criminal, and my mother would have been terribly angry.

[1] Significant nouns have acquired Teutonic capitals by this point. Things must be serious.

I will have to die soon if the Letter arrives. I reckon my days are numbered, quite honestly. That does upset me rather a lot. But I'd rather be dead than a criminal. I never before realised I had so much pride, but it seems I can't let my dignity be hurt. I think perhaps I would do well to die young; I'd never make it in this world. What shall I do in my last days on this earth? I don't think there's anything I really want to do.

I'm accepting the prospect of death rather calmly; I suppose that's the best way to go about it.

I love how teenage diaries are so tight on detail. So many pages in mine – even the secret one – have details like 'Arrived at school 07.35', or 'Bad traffic on the 33 bus route tonight in East Sheen'. To be fair, I needed this diary to blurt out all the rubbish that I couldn't talk to anyone else about, chiefly, it seems, because all the stuff in my head was just so boring.

I began my very secret diary when I was sixteen and in trouble. I'd lost my second London Transport Travelcard. A Travelcard was supposed to last all term and cost ££. If you lost the first one, you could get a replacement for just £, but when you lost that replacement, you had to pay ££ again if you wanted a third one. I didn't have ££: I had p. My mother didn't have ££ either and I knew I was going to be in shit for losing the second one. The morning after losing it I walked to school, six and a half miles, for which I had to get up stupidly early, and that night I forged a new card. I found an old 1987 Travelcard and, with a powerful magnifying glass, paint, and a single-haired paintbrush, I stayed up until the wee hours painstakingly altering the '7' to an '8'. I concentrated so hard that I can still remember doing this incredibly clearly. It worked, and for three weeks I rode around London scot-free. Then I got caught. I had never been in trouble before, except with my mother and my teachers. This was Real-World Trouble.

I WANT CURLY HAIR AND TO BE HAPPY

EMILY LAWLER

This is my first entry thingy and I've decided there's going to be no more bullshit from now on. I think I might actually be able to do this, I will, for the elephants they're cute.[1] I'm only going to write when I feel like it and have the time cos otherwise I will read this in a couple of years and think 'damn I was a boring fuck'.

* * *

I went to the markets and Shirin's birthday which were both pretty cool but I just feel totally depressed. Ashlie lost it to Simon, it really makes me wish I had someone to sleep with. I don't even think I would care if they didn't care about me.

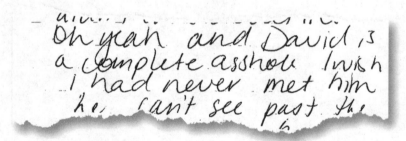

Oh yeah and David is a complete asshole I wish I had never met him. He can't see past the fact that he had to pay to come down here so no matter how he acts I'm supposed to excuse it because he bought a fucking plane ticket? Why are boys such assholes.

I've been loosing it completely recently. I don't know whether I am generally fucked up or it's just being a teenager that makes me upset.

---

[1]My diary at the time had an elephant design.

I really want a boyfriend. I want someone to think I'm sexy and funny and talented and intelligent cos no one else does and it's not right to think that about yourself. I hate my family. I want curly hair and to be happy. Suicide is the only way.

These entries were written in 1999, when I was fifteen. I had moved schools that year from Queensland to New South Wales (both in Australia). The transition was hard and I had trouble fitting in . . . hence the angst.

David was a boy I had liked at my old school. He flew to Sydney to be my formal date. I had really wanted to lose my virginity to him, but he wasn't remotely interested, so I lied to all my friends back home and said that he had tried it on. After this, David didn't want to be my friend any more, which was shocking to me at the time . . . I was outraged that he had had the audacity to say I was ungrateful for him (or rather his parents) paying for the plane ticket to come and be my date. God, I was awful.

AULD LANG SYNE

JANINE ORFORD

> I live in hope, I have such dreams
> and aspirations, that I'd like to
> realise these thoughts like a movie
> ... ... a the screen.

30 December 2001 12.56am

Another year draws to an end. One after the other they play their cruel games.

I live in hope, I have such dreams and aspirations, that I'd like to realise these thoughts like a movie stepping out of the screen.

I would like to make people happy: teachers, friends, parents, but most of all I would like myself to be happy, to watch the corners of my mouth crease upwards, and to beam with sunshine. Maybe.

I'm not, however, starting the year in a fashion I would like, but people place too much importance on New Year's Eve. People sing about Auld Lang Syne, but what has 'it' ever done for me?

I was a huge fan of bad metaphors and decided one day to add them all into one impressive diary entry. At that point I was sixteen and just about to start my final six months of my GCSEs. I'd been quite busy with teenage self-loathing and pity and had left most of my coursework and revision until the very last minute. This, of course, added to my self-loathing and pity and culminated in my writing many cringe-worthy diary entries such as this. Life was such a drag as a teenager, and I must have thought it was a chore to be at the start of another year, when that year would consist mainly of taking exams and being embarrassed by my parents.

ALL HANDS

MAUREEN LEVY

5 May 1974

Went to the dressmaker to try on my bridesmaid dress for Pam's wedding. It's awful and it doesn't suit me and I look so FAT in it. It's sickening. I hate being bridesmaid and having my photo taken + looking so horrible + fat, yugh, I must try + cut down on the calories.

14 May 1974

Went for a fitting with the dressmaker for the bridesmaid dress. All the other bridesmaids are so pretty, + I'm so ugly. I feel dreadful. I'd been building up to this all day and when the dressmaker said 'You should go on a diet, loose some of the spare tyres and go out on grass for a few weeks,' that really did it. I burst into tears + everyone thought it was because of what she said an' it wasn't. I've got such an inferiority complex an' no one ever boosts my ego. I think I'll go into a shell. One thing's sure, I'M NEVER EVER GONNA BE A BRIDESMAID AGAIN – EVER!!!

one thing's sure, I'M NEVER EVER GONNA BE A BRIDESMAID AGAIN EVER!!!

Do dressmakers still exist? Dreadful, warty, opinionated old women. I was a bridesmaid again, but I was in my twenties, and by then able to buy and fit into a dress straight off the rails. I was stunning in shocking pink taffetta (the eighties – a whole other era of fashion).

But in 1974 I had no confidence at all and being fourteen in those days and anything less than skeletal was, as far as my mother was concerned, a crime against humanity and a personal attack on her. Maybe she was right about the second bit . . .

4 June 1974

Valerie told me today that she was going to break it off with David tonight, because she was fed up with him. I hope he's very hurt, just like he hurt me, and I hope that he hates Valerie from now on. I know hes not likely to go with me again cos he hates me, but I hope he doesn't go with anyone.

19 October 1974

David J's party. Nearly 200 people there in a tent in the garden. A boy called Peter asked me to dance . . . ok so I danced with him and got off with him. Nice sort of guy and all that BUT . . . he was all hands . . . and boy do I mean what I say. I didn't know what I was supposed do about it. I nearly died of embarrassment cos he suddenly said look you're all luminous – and I looked down and my bra was glowing through my new green cheesecloth shirt. Cos of the lights and it was awful . . . cos of the hands and boy do I mean hands and the shirt too. HELP!!!

He took my phone number and asked my name and wants to see me again.

I thought I was so grown-up! I knew all about how babies were made. I knew that people kissed. But I never realized that anything else happened in between. Oh my God! I can still remember the sight of my 32A bra, shining like a beacon through my fabulous new cheesecloth shirt.

HAPPY ST PATRICK'S DAY!

NATHAN GUNTER

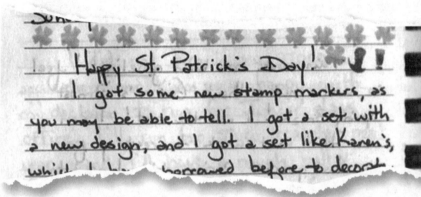

Sunday 17 March 1996
Happy St. Patrick's Day!

I got some new stamp markers, as you may be able to tell. I got a set with a new design, and I got a set like Karen's, which I have borrowed before to decorate this journal, like on March 3rd.

Well, while Spring Break hasn't officially started, I'm resting up anyway. Dad bought the house across the street from his land in Arkansas, and I'm helping him start that grueling moving process.

I know it seems like regression, or simple confusion, but I'm starting to feel something more than acquaintence for Jarrett. I don't know what it is – homosexual attraction? All I know is that: 1.) I'm not feeling it much for Ashlee any more, and 2.) I really like Jarrett, in more ways than one. I am very confused. Extremely.

'Every time I look at you I Go Blind.'

I've been listening to the 'Friends' soundtrack, and in songs like 'I Go Blind,' by Hootie and the Blowfish, 'Good Intentions' by Toad the Wet Sprocket, and especially 'Sexuality' by K.D. Lang I find my

feelings about Jarrett and homosexuality in general mirrored. I wish
one of these damn markers was a question mark. I'd decorate the
whole damn page with it. Maybe I'll be clear by the end of the week!

Anyway –

Dad has bought some calves, and while the side of me that's
'citified' finds them incredibly stupid, a large part of me finds them
cute. I even named a few. There's Madonna, the bitchy one, and
Moesha, the one with an attitude.

This page almost speaks for itself; here I am at age fifteen
wondering if all these 'feelings' I'm having for Jarrett, the all-
American, popular, goofy, football-playing senior who was always
really nice to me, could possibly mean that I was a 'homosexual',
but probably not, and anyway, it shouldn't take me more than a
few days to be clear, and, oh my God, don't you just love my
multicoloured stamp markers? Oh yeah, and I named Dad's new
calves Madonna and Moesha. Good Lord, was anyone ever less
self-aware?

For years after I graduated from high school, whenever I'd run
into someone I knew, they'd all say, 'Oh, we all knew you were gay.
We just never told you.' I wish they had. It also bears mentioning
that I titled my journals back then; this one was 'The Adventures
of Mr. Thing'. Again – speaks for itself.

SWEATY HANDS, BIG KNOCKERS

Helena Burton

Wednesday 14 January 1991

I could kill Louisa, she gets away with too much. Hoxy said my hands were sweaty today, which was true but there's not a lot I can do about it and he didn't have to point it out. Lou also held his hand all the way to the bus stop, which pissed me off coz I had to tag along looking like a right prat.

Tuesday 15 January 1991

Mark said I had big knockers today, which isn't strictly true, but is a lovely compliment anyway.

Well, life hasn't changed much. I still haven't got big knockers and I still get clammy hands on occasion. But I have learnt to tolerate my friends holding hands without wanting to kill them. So that's some progress, I suppose.

OBSESSIONS

X-Men. Cars. The Smiths. Doogie Howser. Don't be ashamed; let your freak flag fly.

ONLY THE SMITHS ARE IMPORTANT

PIP HAWKES

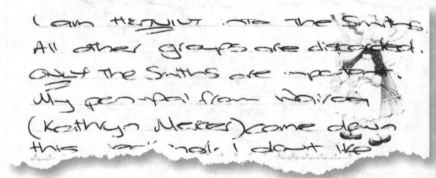

Wednesday 19 October 1988

*I am HEAVILY into The Smiths. All other groups are discarded.
ONLY The Smiths are important. Kate and I went out to Napier on
Saturday – and I bought two new Morrissey posters from the EMI
shop. I've never seen Morrissey or Smiths posters before – so I was
VERY happy. They're both black and white and rather big. I also have
another colour Smiths poster that Shelley bought me back from
Australia. I love it.*

*Okay – since before going to America – I've always liked Stephen
Keatley – I'll see if I've mentioned him before. Yes – I have. On the 13
of August. He was in my Economics class. But there were 40 people so
the class got split into two – and unfortunately he was put in the other
one. Anyway – he used to give letters to James (his friend who is in my
Economics class) who passed them onto me. In the 1st letter he sent
two tapes and a 2 page letter. I was very happy! One cassette was a
live Smiths one from Amsterdam in 1984 and the other was blank
and he wanted me to tape 'Louder Than Bombs'. I didn't because it's a*

compilation – so instead I taped Darrens 12" B-sides. Anyway – now Stephen POSTS letters to me – and I post back. The latest one I got was 2 days ago – and it was was 14 pages long. (It was 2 letters, one 4 pages and one 10). He is just like a Junior version of Morrissey. I like everything about Morrissey – most of all – his celibacy! Oh hang on – I thought celibacy was not having sex – but it's actually being unmarried and having a single life – no – that CAN'T be right! I plan on getting married (maybe) but not having children – remaining a virgin – oh god – it sounds like I want to be a nun!

Stephen is very nice! Today was mufti day and he'd died his hair . . . BLACK!!! But it comes out when you wash it – and he'd wet it to make it stick up and the dye ran down his hands – so I only saw it when it was half black and half his natural reddy/brown. Two letters ago he confessed to liking me and I was very happy. But now people at school are beginning to find out and it's becoming rather embarrassing. We plan to 'ACTUALLY' meet soon! At the cemetary. I'm dreading it – he's very deep and I'm not as deep as him. He thinks I'm VERY intelligent – but I don't think I'm intelligent as he thinks. He is also shy to meet me – so maybe we won't for a while – I suggested we should keep writing for longer.

As I've said before – I HATE Glenda! Although I haven't hung round with her until I last said. She STILL copies me! I've told her my feelings to her face before – but they have no effect. So I decided last Friday to write her a note. It was kind of weird and not very nice. Anyway – she showed it to her mother and her mother thinks that anyone capable of writing that note must be in a state of melancholy, have a major complex, be mentally deprived and insane!! Ha Ha!

Well – I always KNEW I wasn't QUITE normal! I quite happily agree with those anyway, but not the 'mentally deprived' one!! I feel like writing a REALLY strange note! So they think I'm TOTALLY cracked!

I've made a real mess of my hair! On Thursday (nearly 2 weeks ago) I shaved a HUGE patch behind and above my ear – also I cut a VERY big chunk off the top of my head so I now have a short, spiky tuft! I also cut off the other ear lots of short bits and the most noticeable thing is this chunk out of the back. When you walk past people – they sometimes stare! Although I quite enjoy the attention – I want people to think I'm strange! And to respect me for it – most people in my class respect me for it – in fact they wholly encourage it! When my bald patch grows back I'm getting my hair cut. It will be about this long _____ at the sides – layered and short at the back and with a long punky fringe. I wish to be a mongrel – a mix between these 4 groups, a punk, goths, trendies and my normally weird self. By 'trendy' I mean cycling shorts etc. I deeply admire punks and goths! I like the punk image but a gothic personality.

At school now Chrissie and Kirsten hang round with us – I like them – 'specially Chrissie. I would love to be her friend! Shes so nice! And she greatly respects me. She smokes – but it doesn't make any difference. I got a letter today from Kathryn – it was mainly about Darren. I'll have to reply soon – but I want to write another letter to Stephen. I started it yesterday and I wrote one the day before which I posted – and I'll post this one when I get a reply from him. I feel VERY lucky!! I've just decided – well – not decided – but found out – I'm nihilistic! God – Dad's just come in and told me to tidy my room – it is BLOODY TIDY!! He must have had a bad day at work – WANKER.

So this was written at age fourteen, when I was obviously a big fan of exclamation marks and dashes . . . I did eventually ACTUALLY meet Stephen (yes, at the cemetery) after approximately four months of correspondence.

The first photo, with my double tape deck, was taken two months after this diary entry. And in the second picture you can see the advances I'd made working on my look.

You'll be pleased to know that I continue to command respect from my peers, as I've had twenty years since this diary entry to perfect my look and develop my normal weirdness. Apologies to my poor tidy dad.

CARS

JED PAPPAS

Wroke off Dad's car today. Jamma and I borrowed it to burn around Fishguard square but I overcooked it in fourth around cross corner and over-steered into a gate. Rear of the car completely squashed, bum ... ina on the ground. Mira...

8 September 1989

Wrote off Dad's car today. Jamma and I borrowed it to burn around Fishguard square but I overcooked it in fourth around Cross Corner and over steered into a gate. Rear of the car completely squashed, bumper was hanging on the ground. Miraculously, managed to drive it home leading a trail of sparks. I backed it into the space so that the damage wasn't immediately visible and then Jamma said 'Can you give us a lift up the hill?' to which I replied rather aghast 'Fuck off, Jamma, we just barely managed to get the bloody thing home?' He really can be a dozy bugger sometimes. Went and told Dad, and much to my surprise he took it rather well. 'It probably isn't a write-off' he muttered as we walked down to assess the damage. Looking at the front he said 'Its not too bad, son' and then moved on to the back and soon changed his tune, once he observed the accordion where the boot used to be. 'Mmm' he murmured and then said 'What are we going to tell your mother?' Hearing these words and seeing the chance of an escape from my deserved fate, I quickly replied 'How about the Irish Gypsies nicked it!' However, Dad after giving it some thought said 'No son, I think you better tell her the truth' Bugger! Mum, of course went spare, I offered to buy a new car and I was grounded again. Next time, I'll take it in third and won't lift off.

14 November 1989

Lyd [my sister, Lydia] shunted Mum's car last night. It's only the fender that is damaged, but Mum wasn't too pleased, she lamented in true biblical fashion 'What have I done to deserve such terrible kids!' I asked Lyd what happened and she said that the seat was too low and she couldn't see properly over the bonnet and therefore didn't see Newport wall until she was bouncing off it. However, I suspect it had more to do with the half a dozen VAT's [vodka and tonics] I saw her neck back in the Globe [Pub].

4 February 1990

Picked up the Capri today. Went down with Mum and handed over the 350 for it. Really wanted that TR7, but not too disappointed. It's pretty quick, managed to get it to step out on me around the harbour roundabout. Drove up to Llanwnda to show Jamma and we took it for a spin to Pwllgwaelodd. Had a few pints and then did a few doughnuts in the car park. Managed to get a ton 5 out of it down the Garn Gelli, but I think it will do more.

1 March 1990

Grounded again last night and banned from using the car. But am totally indignant by the whole injustice of it all!! I finished work at about three and then went out for a few pints with Ken. Then we met up with Dai James and then went on a pub crawl. I was hanging. All I remember is leaving the Coach House and making my way home, pretty early about 9 o'clock. However, my memory is a little sketchy but I do remember walking across the parrog[1] and finding myself in the middle of the road without meaning it, collapsing under the spider[2], puking and sleeping for a while and crawling on my knees up the water walk[3]. When I did make it home, apparently

---

[1] The harbour area of Newport.
[2] The spider' was a climbing frame in a children's playground shaped like a spider.
[3] The water walk was a footpath that led from my house down the mountainside into the village centre. A stream ran off the mountain and flowed parallel to the footpath.

5 hours later, Mum and Lyd were waiting up for me. 'You're Drunk!' Mum said in disgust. I stood up straight and replied with all the dignity I could muster 'Of course I'm drunk, mother, I have just spent the whole night crawling home!' and then span on my heels and marched out into the hallway. However, I tripped up the stairs and lay there nose to carpet until Lyd came and carried me to bed. But I'm totally fucked off with being banned from using my car. I did the decent thing, I left it in Fishguard. I couldn't walk let alone drive and I did the right thing. The punishment doesn't fit the crime.

7 July 1990
Rolled the bread van today. Had to do Sharon's round as she was sick, so loaded the van and went down the Gwaun [Valley]. Went a bit quick down by Bessies[4] and ended up leaving the road, clipping a phone box and flipping into a field. Might have passed out, not sure, but next thing I remember is being on my side covered in current buns. Phoned Richard to come and pull me out. He came and after much laughter, put me right way up and towed me to the road. I assessed the damage. Wholewheats were unscathed, Tea cakes scattered, Tins scuffed, Eclairs mangled and custard slices, completely fucked! Managed to drive it back to the bakery. Ken saw the funny side, until Sue reminded him that it wasn't very funny at all. Got sent home, no pay. Bummer!

5 November 1990
A very sad day indeed. Lyd wrote off the Capri today. She woke me early and after stealing some more fags asked to borrow the car as her's wouldn't start. Before I could answer, she was gone and so was my keys. Went to school but got a call mid morning to return home as my sister had been involved in an accident. Went home and found Lyd in a neck brace, looking very sheepish indeed. Dad told me that the car had been towed back to Wern road and I could see it if I wanted.

---

[4] Bessie's was a rural pub in Pontfaen, a small village in the Gwaun Valley, and officially titled The Dyffren Arms, where an old lady would serve you through a hatch with a jug of her home brew.

Went down and saw the remains of the Capri. The front was completely smashed in and the bonnet buckled, the back was buggered and one of the sides wasn't too flash either. As I learned tonight, she was doing about 70 down into Wolf's castle and hit some black ice and ended up smashing into one wall and then bouncing off and then ploughing into the opposite one. Although, I am still pissed off at Lyd, I must admit there is a little tinge of relief and admiration. Relief as I know it was only a matter of time before I did it myself and maybe would not have been so lucky and admiration because 'Fair dues, it was a bloody good shunt!'

Cars. They have always been my Achilles heel. For some it was women; for me, cars. I was sixteen when the diary starts (seventeen when it ends), newly arrived back to West Wales from two years of high school in America. I had taught myself to drive by watching television and reading racing magazines and as a result was always attempting to find the limits of anything I drove. I am now a television producer for a major motor-racing series.

DARLENE

HOLLY BURNS

> Dear Sara,
>
> This is probably strange getting fan mail
> from a girl, but i just wanted to say 'hi' and
> how i think you're really great on the show. i
> can't believe you work with Johnny Galecki. what's
> he like? seriously, i am so addicted to your show,
> cos i live in England the TV isn't that great, and
> 'Roseanne' the best programme i've watched ever!

Haslemere, Surrey
ENGLAND

Dear Sara,
This is probably strange getting fan mail from a girl, but I just wanted
to say 'hi' and how I think you're really great on the show. I can't
believe you work with Johnny Galecki! What's he like? Seriously, I am
so addicted to your show. Cos I live in England the TV isn't that great,
and 'Roseanne' is the best programme I've watched ever!

I can't believe you guys (well, Darlene and David) split up on the
show. Sorry, I know I'm talking as if you really ARE Darlene in real
life, but it really feels like it, it feels like I know you as a friend. You
see, I'm having some problems right now with a friend and a guy, and
it feels like you are sort of a role model, someone I can talk to and
relate to. Sorry, I'm talking crap – I'm sorry if I'm boring you to death
– I just need to talk to someone and you're so much like me on
the show and . . . I'm sorry, I know people aren't their
characters on TV but you just seem so great
and perfect and funny and I feel like I know
you – like you're a big sister or something. I'm
not screwed up, really, although this letter does

By air mail
Par avion

imply that I am. Put it down if you want, it's a load of crap – I need a friend. OK, I like this guy, I like him a lot – well, everyone does – he's gorgeous, funny, popular etc. I saw him at a BBQ at the beginning of summer and I thought he kinda liked me, then I saw him in September – very briefly. After that, I found out he'd been with one of my close friends all night at a party – OK he's not mine or anything, but this friend knew I really, really liked him. Some of my friends say he likes me and I really want it to be true, and they say I should write to him. I really want to write to him or SOMETHING, but I don't know what to write or do or anything.

> I'm also having problems with one of my best friends but I don't want to bore you with that, so I won't go into it.

I'm also having problems with one of my best friends but I don't want to bore you with that, so I won't go into it.

Look, Sara, I'm really sorry for writing all this crap to you, I just needed to talk, and I feel like I know you (or Darlene should I say) like a friend; no, better than one of my friends. I'm really sorry if I've wasted your time. I hope you don't think I'm screwed up.

Love,
Holly xxx

This is a fan letter I wrote (and thankfully never posted) to Sara Gilbert, who played Darlene on *Roseanne*, and with whom I was slightly obsessed. I wrote from boarding school, asking relationship advice. It goes on and on. I still have the envelope, with its three sweetly hopeful airmail stickers. I see I didn't even bother with a city or state, so certain was I that 'Miss S. Gilbert, 10000 Santa Monica Boulevard, USA' would be enough to get it to her.

BOYS

MELISSA GATES

June 1983

25 Saturday
WEEK 25 (176-189)   O Full Moon

[handwritten diary entry] woke up lay around talking to Lisa, got up got ready had breakfast, dressed up, and I mean up spiky hair, plaits, all in black, very ace ... hats et

Saturday 25 June 1983

Woke up, lay around talking to Lisa, got up, got ready, had breakfast, dressed up, and I mean up – spiky hair, plaits, all in black. Very ace, looking weird, hats etc, very def. Eventually got the bus. On the very long way there 2 lovely boys got on, very wierd looking – dyed, razored, curly hair. Yum yum, they kept looking at us. We got off the bus, they followed us into Square[1]. They waved, they went out of Square, we followed, they followed us, then the taller one came up and said 'Excuse me, my mate wants to know, are you following us, or are we following you?' We chatted. I was nervous. They were really lovely. Yum yum. My dream boys – absolutely lovely – Vince Clark and Martin Gore [from Depeche Mode]. Yum yum. We talked, we told them we were 15.[2] They didn't question it! It was really ego boosting. Paul had a Thompson Twins tattoo on his arm and Phil had a lovely coat. Paul was a prat, always dancing around, poking me. Very weird – lovely. Went around with them hardly believeing two lovely blokes like them would fancy us. Paul was 19 and Phil (the super gorgeous one all in black, black, blonde and orange hair, 5 ear pierce holes, black baggies, Japanese t-shirt, long coat etc) was 18. Yum yum. Lost

[1] Square was a shop in Bath that sold underground designer clothes and fash mags like *iD* – our bible at the time.
[2] We were thirteen!

them but later met up with them. The conversation wasn't exactly exciting. Paul pratted about – in the end we got on the bus and they sat apart from us, talking to some other girls. But they did keep on looking. I overheard Paul saying 'I really like her – yeah, she's alright' (looking at me). The girl said 'You are stupid, you should've asked her to get off with you.' They got off, said 'see ya, see ya at Thompson Twins, bye' and were gone. We sat and were depressed, Lisa and me. Lisa told me Paul really fancied me, but we both definitely liked Phil the best, yum yum. I still can't believe it happened, I can't believe I'm so lucky, I feel so big BIG[3] now. My ego is a bit inflated. Harry is nothing compared to them.[4] I should've got a photo of them. Got home, were both upset cos we'll probably never see them again. Lisa went, had tea, watched TV. Did it really happen? Thank you God!!!

I was a teenage goth. It was 1983 when I first started to morph from a nice little girl who loved ballet and her pet rabbits to a sulky slut with black back-combed hair and ripped tights. Looking back I mainly feel astonishment and gratitude that my parents were so understanding about it. My dad would dutifully drive the half-hour or so from Devizes to Chippenham to pick me and my 'friend' Lisa up from the alternative disco. The inverted commas are there because, in common with a lot of intense teenage girls given to writing poetry, we principally viewed each other as competition and often hated each other. Many diary entries detail my pain at feeling she'd betrayed or eclipsed me – getting off with some boy I'd liked first or just managing to get her hair spikier than mine.

[3] This is underlined three times. I've practically gone through the paper I was pressing so hard with my biro.
[4] Previous object of my desire to whom I'd never spoken. A Chinese boy with a wedge haircut and David Bowie 'Let's Dance' style pleated trousers ordered from those small ads at the back of the *NME*. My older brother used to go break-dancing with him and other mates on a bit of cardboard in the market square of Devizes.

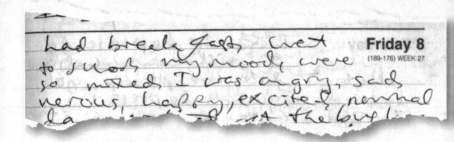

Had breakfast, went to school. My moods were so mixed, I was angry, sad, nervous, happy, excited. Normal day. Got the bus home with Lisa, we were both moody and just to add to my problems I was on. Got ready, excited and nervous. I looked brilliant, sat around, sooo nervous, Zoe and Hayley picked us up. All the way there I was so nervous. Got out the car and I heard whistles and 'Hey!' – we saw who was sitting outside the pub across the road – Paul and Phil! I was sooo happy.

Friday 8 July 1983

Had breakfast, went to school. My moods were so mixed, I was angry, sad, nervous, happy, excited. Normal day. Got the bus home with Lisa, we were both moody and just to add to my problems I was on. Got ready, excited and nervous. I looked brilliant, sat around, sooo nervous, Zoe and Hayley picked us up. All the way there I was so nervous. Got out the car and I heard whistles and 'Hey!' – we saw who was sitting outside the pub across the road – Paul and Phil! I was sooo happy. We went across the road but they didn't seem to be so pleased to meet us, we didn't talk much, the conversation was stilted. We went back across the road and stood in the queue, but they practically ignored us. They were chatting up a few other girls. We were sooo let down, deflated. We talked to Hayley and Zoe who were really nice. We waited in the queue for ages, and then Phil started talking to me again. He insulted my earrings, dress, hair, wristband etc. They were really nasty. We chatted a lot more. Phil put his arms around me and we stood really close, but I knew then that they are both just big flirts. The old love I saw in Paul's eyes had gone – only disinterest. We went in and Paul got close to me. He went upstairs with us, but went down again cos Phil was downstairs.[5] Lisa and me were sooo bitter. We sat in the dark arguing, snapping – trying not to be too depressed. It was obvious we meant almost nothing to them. The support group came on – Black. They were brilliant. The lead singer was cute. The music was very good. Then the Thompson Twins came on. They were really great – much better than any live show I've seen. I really would have enjoyed it if it

[5] The venue, Golddiggers, in Chippenham, was over-eighteens downstairs, and allowed underage punters in for gigs upstairs, where only fizzy pop was served. No self-respecting over-eighteen-year-old would be seen dead up there, hence our mortification.

hadn't been for those bloody two boys. They sat up on the stage and were really joining in. Upstairs all the people sat in silence, listening. How boring. Lisa and me clapped our hearts out. Oh, if only I was 18. Oh god, I wish I was 18. It all went really slowly. I found myself wishing everyone would go away. The Thompson Twins finished. They really seemed to care about us before, but now . . .[6] Afterwards we all stood outside. Lisa and me went up and talked to Paul but he seemed so disinterested. Lisa was being bitchy and then, oh my God, my Dad came up. Oh my God, Phil came up, grinning, expecting a lift. I waved him away whispering 'Piss off'. He looked amused. We got in the car and I couldn't believe what I'd done. How childish, pathetic. Oh no. I just kicked myself sooo much. Oh no. We got home, went to bed. Lisa wasn't herself, so I cried myself to sleep.

For years, before I dared open them, I liked to imagine that these diaries would reveal a tortured soul, sensitive and philosophically inclined. In fact, like most thirteen-year-old girls, the thing that seems to occupy my every waking thought is boys. That was what I was obsessed with really, not death. Lisa and I used to get the bus to Bath most Saturdays to look at clothes and records, but mainly to look at boys. This entry charts one of the first times we actually talked to some. As you can imagine, the diary entries not reproduced here detailed endlessly long, pointless days at school filled with longing and fear.

[6] Clearly I'm talking about Paul and Phil here, not the Thompson Twins . . .

DOOGIE HOWSER

JOHANNA GOHMANN

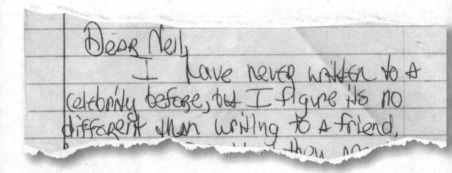

Dear Neil,
I have never written to a celebrity before, but I figure it's no different than writing to a friend, besides the fact that they aren't teen idols and don't receive fan mail, what's the difference, right?

Now, I'm not writing because I want your underwear or a lock of your hair, or anything goofy like that. I just wanted to tell you that I respect you a lot both as an actor and a person. I act a lot myself, and I enjoy watching how you interpret your Doogie character every week. I have seen you on various talk shows and have read a couple articles, and it seems to me that you are one funny and classy guy.

But I must admit, the first time I watched your show I only did so because my friend kept telling me how good it was, and I read somewhere that you and I share one of the same favorite actors, John Lithgow. So I figured, anybody that likes John Lithgow (there aren't an over abundance of people that do) can't be all that bad. So I watched. And I was very impressed. Your Doogie is a very believable one, and now your show has become one of the few shows I watch steadily every week (I'm more of a movie fan, myself).

Well, I know what with your series and fan mail, you haven't got a lot of time for small time actresses like myself, but if your mother or secretary or whoever helps with your fan mail, if you could manage it,

I'd LOVE an autographed picture! Congratulations on your success, and I wish you luck in the future.

Sincerely yours,

Jo Gohmann

P.S. Tell Abby Wolfe she's one lucky gal!

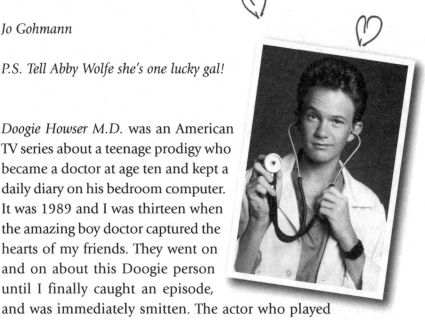

Doogie Howser M.D. was an American TV series about a teenage prodigy who became a doctor at age ten and kept a daily diary on his bedroom computer. It was 1989 and I was thirteen when the amazing boy doctor captured the hearts of my friends. They went on and on about this Doogie person until I finally caught an episode, and was immediately smitten. The actor who played Doogie, Neil Patrick Harris, was everything a small-town girl on the cusp of puberty could want: cherub-faced, devoid of body hair, and gay.

I fell pretty hard, and not only penned a fan letter, I actually sent it (the equivalent to sending a fan letter to Ant and Dec during their *Byker Grove* era). I know for a fact that I sent it because six years later a forwarded postcard from the Neil Patrick Harris Fan Club turned up in my mailbox. It featured a glossy photo of Neil, and a short message updating me on his current career plans. Naturally, my college friends assumed someone had signed me up for the club as a joke. They all had a good laugh, and I chuckled right along with them, pretending to wonder who on earth would DO such a thing.

X-MEN

NINA GOTUA

The unbearable pain of a television ban and my obsession with the *X-Men*. I moved to the UK from Yugoslavia, via Holland, with my mum when I was twelve, which put me within the reaches of my maternal Grandmother – a woman whose chief crime was taking what I considered to be an excessive interest in my life, physical well-being and the clutter in my room. My defence of rolling my eyes expressively would irritate the Grandmother beyond measure, which would in turn fire up my mother to react with some Inhumane Punishment (such as a television ban).

Since, at the time, a separation from my favourite programme rendered my life meaningless, I felt I had no choice but to see my grandmother as the housecoated harbinger of ultimate doom and blame her for my inner torment.

When faced with the combined tyranny of family members expecting me to be courteous to them and teachers expecting me to do homework, television seemed to be my only logical escape. Surely movies and cartoons would equip me with all the knowledge and skills I would need to prosper in the world!

This particular gem of an entry also contains the diary version of Twitter: 'Must get toilet paper; getting it; got it'.

Thursday 10 March 1994

Dear diary,
There is one cartoon on TV that I really love. It is called X-men. Now,
supposedly I've been impolite to the Grandmother and my mother has
grounded me, so now I can't even watch it, or even tape it. I don't
think she knows how much she had hurt me. I don't think she cares. I
don't think anybody cares. Maybe that's what she wanted to do, hurt
me. Well, she certainly did succeed. She can be proud now. When she

and the Grandmother were gone I sat down and cried like I haven't cried in a long time. She keeps punishing me for every little thing I do. I don't know, I guess I just need to let it all out, to tell someone. Damn the Grandmother! It's all her fault! It has to be! If it wasn't for her, I would still be able to watch the X-Men. I can't let the mother know I cried! She would probably just punish me again. She just doesn't understand. I don't think she ever will. I need to sneak out and get more toilet paper to blow my nose. I guess it's not fair me blaming the Grandmother, but I guess I need to blame someone. Tears don't seem to stop. They just keep on coming, and the more I write the more upset I get. I'm going to get that toilet paper now. Mission complete. Toilet paper with me now. I know I should be more mature and responsible, Indians would not cry, but I guess even 13 year old girls have a right to be upset and lonely, just like I am. It's a big tough world, and I'm lonely and scared. I've got a real bad headache, probably from crying so much. But every once in a while I need to let the tears out. I keep my emotions in myself for too long. Maybe I'll start smoking soon, while my organs are still developing. That would serve mother right. I could get sick, and get lung cancer and she would be stuck without someone to punish. I wonder if it would ruin her satisfaction if I didn't show at all that she hurt me. But I'm going to the Rocky Mountains to live with the Indians, where no one can punish me again.

again.

> Mother says that she is hurting ten thousand more times than me, when I'm hurting. Well, I'm hurting now, but I'm pretty positive that she isn't. I'm feeling so lonely,

Mother says that she is hurting ten thousand more times than me, when I'm hurting. Well, I'm hurting now, but I'm pretty positive *that she isn't. I'm feeling so lonely, so disappointed. It's been such a long time since I cried. Maybe that's why I'm crying so much now.*

I don't know why I'm so upset. I mean after all it's just a cartoon. But I like it so much! It isn't fair at all.

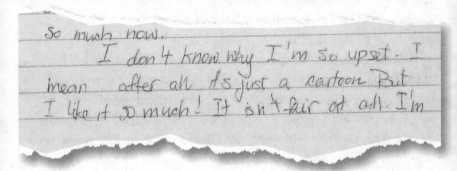

So much now.
I don't know why I'm so upset. I mean after all it's just a cartoon. But I like it so much! It isn't fair at all. I'm

In the following entry, driven mad by *X-Men*less despair, I hatch outlandish schemes designed to make my mother finally give in and retract the punishment of ultimate doom. Although I'm not sure how exactly banging my head against the wall was going to advance my cause, unless they played *X-Men* in unconsciousness.

11 March 1993
The X-Men are mutants and they use their powers to work on humans and mutants living in peace. But they do a lot of fighting too. What really draws me to this cartoon are the characters, I guess. I must find a way to watch the X-Men.

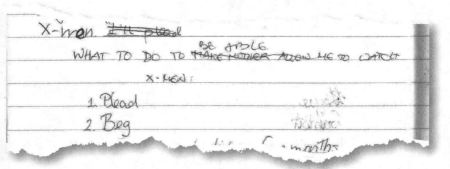

WHAT TO DO TO BE ABLE TO WATCH X-MEN:

1. *Plead*
2. *Beg*
3. *Offer to wash dishes for 2 months*
4. *Bring home good grades*
5. *Throw myself at her feet and plea*
6. *Offer to do all the ironing around the house*
7. *Commit suicide (maybe they have cable in heaven)*
8. *Offer to do all the cooking (probably would taste better than hers, anyway)*
9. *Kick and scream (she'll want to rest)*
10. *Cry (maybe she'll take pity)*
11. *Despair (maybe she'll take pity)*
12. *Bang my head against the wall*
13. *Run away to some friendly person who has cable or satellite, so that I may watch the X-Men*
14. *Offer to be nicer to Ivan [my cousin]*
15. *Offer to be nicer to Grandmother*
16. *Blackmail her*
17. *Get married to someone with cable*
18. *Win a contest that offers as a big prize all tapes of X-Men*
19. *Ask someone else to tape it for me*
20. *Get sick with X-Men as the only cure that can save me*

Victory! She's gonna tape the X-men for me! Oh Gawd I'm so happy. She even allowed me to watch TV again.

ORCHESTRA

LIZ BANKS

This is the tale of a fifteen-year-old second violin's crush on a clarinettist two years her senior. I went to an all-girls school and the only opportunity to meet boys was when we did extracurricular activities with the all-boys school nearby. I offer this as some kind of excuse for my utter teenage hopelessness.

Wednesday ~~18th April~~ May
You'll never guess in a million years what has happened today. [blank] took me on one side at lunchtime – she hasn't heard my denials – she told [blank] and said that it was recieved favourably and that he couldn't believe that I could like him even though [blank] was winding him up. [blank] suggested he get to know me informall.. - coffee at the weekend or something.
~vedve..

Wednesday 13 May
You'll never guess in a million years what has happened today. Lucy [flute] took me on one side at lunchtime – she hasn't heard my denials – she told Adrian [clarinet] and said that it was received favourably and that he couldn't believe that I could like him and thought Lucy was winding him up. Lucy suggested he get to know me informally, go out for coffee at the weekend or something.[1]

I didn't really ask her any pertinent questions, I was in shock, come on! I believe her, why would she lie? Or perhaps she would. How can he like me? I'm hardly Venus am I? He's 17 for Christ's sake.

I haven't told anyone, I've just been grinning to myself all afternoon. My stomach's all knotted up. It's so odd. I've got to ask Lucy tomorrow exactly what she said to him and – she asked me whether I would go out – informally – with him for coffee, she was going to

[1] There was no Starbucks in my rural English market town in 1992, so I'm not quite sure where this cosmopolitan meeting of mid-teens was going to take place.

arrange it I think and I said no but I think I'll accept. Why not? We could just get to know each other. What the hell does he think of me? How will I tell my friends I've been lying to them. Oh God.

Washed hair.

Did very little work.

School photo.

God, what is going to happen? I've got <u>orchestra</u> tomorrow. I've got to ask him if he can go to the next meeting [that would be the Debating Society Committee meeting] *and what if he mentions what Lucy has said to him? What if she hasn't really said anything? I really can't believe this.*

Thursday 14 May

The thick plottens. I got hold of Lucy at lunchtime. She had spoken to Adrian after the AGM (which means he knew at the committee meeting) and had dropped some subtle hints (!) He had said 'It's Liz, isn't it?' How did he know? Anyway Lucy had asked him whether he was interested and he said he was. He can't believe I see anything – and I can't believe he sees anything at all in me. Anyway she had suggested to him that he get to know me informally: this Saturday. She's trying to get him to phone me. She says he's a lovely person and she likes me and she thought as we both liked each other it was stupid not to try and if it doesn't work it's not for want of trying. I saw, I spoke to him, at orchestra – I asked if he could get to the next meeting (which is about as far as my flirting goes!) He's so old looking. I mean, I'm only a girl and he's 17. I don't mind but why doesn't he? I still haven't told anyone.

I've been anxious about the phone ringing. It hasn't and if he doesn't at all I shall probably be disappointed but that's silly because we've got a whole year and Saturday's so soon. What would we talk about, I'd probably clam up. No, worse, I'd be entirely stupid. I really can't believe he thinks I'm good looking – he must do. It's mind boggling. I've spent the whole day smiling at everyone.

He could be thinking of me now. Me, I can't believe that anyone can care about me.

Washed hair.

Did the 'racial purity' bit of my history homework.

I don't know whether I shall tell my friends. It's hard to keep to myself but I don't really know how to put it.

Lucy's last day of school tomorrow [before exam leave for her A-levels]. *She's been really nice to me – I mean I'm only a little 4th former and not a particularly nice one at that. I like her. I hope she does well.*

Friday 15 May

It's only ten to five but I've got to get this off my chest. Disappointment is not the word for it. I feel stupid and small and I'm never going to be able to face Adrian again. Jenny [saxophone] *told me this morning – dear old Jen – I really don't like her a morsel – that Adrian had been talking to her sister* [also clarinet] *at orchestra. He thought I was 'a nice girl' and had 'a healthy interest in sport'(?!) but he didn't fancy me. So Jen's sister knows now and I was a fool to think anything was going to happen. Part of me is hoping he will ring tonight but I know he won't (even though today is my Just Seventeen lucky day!) I feel so down and stupid. Stupid, stupid. I'm crushed really, that's all he had to do. There is the question still of who do I believe Lucy or Jenny's sister but he could have changed his mind. He's known since the AGM, saw me at committee meeting and didn't like me after all. Good job I didn't tell my friends but Jenny acted like I had no feelings – Helen heard and she laughed. People think I've got no feelings at all. I feel awful. I hope Adrian's pleased with himself.*

Now of course I am down on myself and see even more that nobody could ever see anything in me. I suppose he said that to Jenny's sister so I'd hear and be 'let down gently'. How stupid I am. I can't see him again.

On the other hand, I've got a year to work on it.

It's now 10 to midnight. What the hell was Lucy talking about? He's not the least bit interested in me at all and Jenny was right. How can I see him again. It is indeed embarrassing to have your feelings made public which is why I kept them to myself. He does not find me physically attractive. I don't like looking in the mirror (Can I forgive him for giving Jenny a reason to mock me?) I think that's the least he could do, he's nothing special himself, he should be damn glad that someone fancies him. I know I would be.

Sunday 23 August

Back home. Depressed. Dad just came in and found me crying but he couldn't help.

> *Why am I unhappy?*
> *Because mum and dad row*
> *Because I have school work to do*
> *Because Rob Andrew* [England Rugby Union Fly Half] *and Graeme Hick* [England and Worcestershire batsman] *are married*
> *Because I have GCSEs next year*
> *Because I am ugly*
> *Because Adrian didn't fancy me*
> *Because I've done no art* [I was referring to art homework, rather than art generally. I think.]
> *Because I have no friends I like*
> *Because my room's a mess*
> *Because there's a Conservative government.*

POETRY

You have feelings! You have yearnings! You have a thesaurus!

THE ARC LIGHT OF INSANITY

NICK HUGHES

9 June 1985

Death after life

Idea – an illusion – fading, no, taking hold
Something – Something's wrong. I'm – I'm cold
People – downstairs – lost in my desert, lost –
Writhing but living – talking, breathing, lost.

Reach – they can't reach – pulling, pulling
Inside, pulling inside – you, it's you – you
Can't touch, too far removed from thought, but
I think, and I'm real, you can't see, you can't feel

The arc light of insanity dazzles me slightly
The jack boots of convention hurt my swollen toes
The prison of loneliness again slams its door
In the elevator of direction I can't find my floor

Watch me fall
Won't somebody pay some attention
Hear me call
Only death comes afterlife's way

Goodbye, I'll leave you
I have no heart to tease you
But I think you'll find
You can't look in your mind
And I know you'll discover
When you can no longer recover
Only death comes after life

Sharproom prelude:

Colours spill bright from the twilight mind
Of a lost lonely medium with hands sadly lined.
The feeling of ~~our~~ love no longer can linger
in the heart of a ~~prodigy~~ fool with hope on each finger
^ . . . . child of the evening

19 September 1985

Sharp room prelude
─────────────────

Colours spill bright from the twilight mind
Of a lost lonely medium with hands sadly lined.
The feeling of love no longer can linger
in the heart of a ~~prodigy~~ fool with hope on each finger
A vision of light, a child of the evening
Homeless helpless hapless, devoid of a meaning
For what is life passed, as I laugh or I cry
If not a worthless shell in which I have lied

These horrific verses were written when I was sixteen or so, and were originally intended to be lyrics for songs that never got written. They pay homage to my musical heroes of that time, who included Pink Floyd, IQ and (particularly) Marillion (whose own lyrics at the time wouldn't be out of place in a volume like this). There's a great deal of self-loathing in what I will hilariously call 'my work' around this time, but it was just a pose; I was really quite optimistic in those days. I found them on loose pages stuck into my actual diaries of that time (which I'm not even prepared to glance at sideways, let alone allow to be published).

I don't actually cringe too much re-reading them; I think they're highly amusing, and I'm happy that I can look back at that teenager, smugly satisfied that I'm a proper grown-up now. Sometimes.

WHEN YOUR MOON SHINES RED

CAMILLA YOUNG

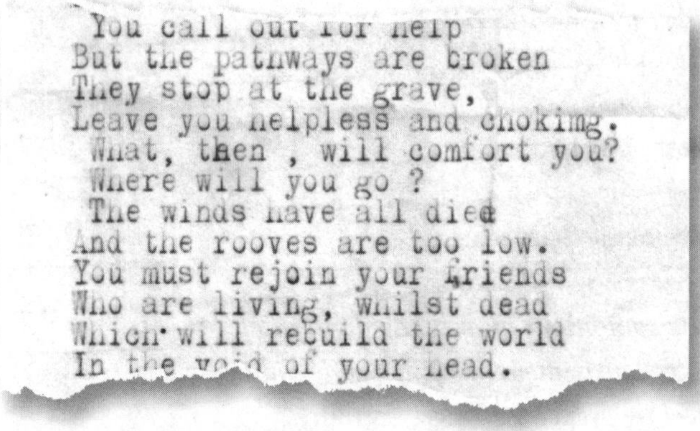

You call out for help
But the pathways are broken
They stop at the grave,
Leave you helpless and chokimg.
What, then , will comfort you?
Where will you go ?
The winds have all died
And the rooves are too low.
You must rejoin your friends
Who are living, whilst dead
Which will rebuild the world
In the void of your head.

So where will you go
When your moon shines red?
What will you do
When your friends are dead?
The world will be pointless
The lines will be shattered
You convince yourself blindly
That none of it mattered.
You call out for help
But the pathways are broken
They stop at the grave,
Leave you helpless and chokimg.
What, then, will comfort you?
Where will you go?
The winds have all died
And the rooves are too low.
You must rejoin your friends
Who are living, whilst dead
Which will rebuild the world
In the void of your head.

✳✳✳

She sits on the rug
And her dress spreads around her
Their laughter
And their smiles surround her.
She smiles, and her eyes
Carry the innocence
Of a three-year-old child
Daughter of insignificance
But briefly she turned her head
And her eyes caught mine
With the look of a hundred years,
The look of infinite time . . .
Then she's away, running, laughing
Over the hill, through the flowers
Similarly I watch as she runs from the truth
Finds her own world and cowers.

✳✳✳

I tried to fly
but you were the anchor
you weighed me down
and my wings were broken.
I wanted to be
free from the people
the world and life

and everything.
But you insist
You keep me down
Oblivious to my
Needs and screams.
Either I die first
Never once free
Or you have to realise
The crying in me.

These are three of the poems I wrote in 1996 when I was supposed to be working for my GCSEs. I wrote lots of poetry, fuelled by my alter ego who refused to advance beyond the age of three until everyone gave her lots of attention and who spent most of her time running through fields of flowers with a beatific smile on her face. However beneath the beatific smile lurked a dreadfully misunderstood creature whose soul was rent asunder (and would stay that way until given lots of attention). I wrote everything on an old-fashioned typewriter, because of its great literary authority.

LIKE AN ALBATROSS

ALEX BARCLAY

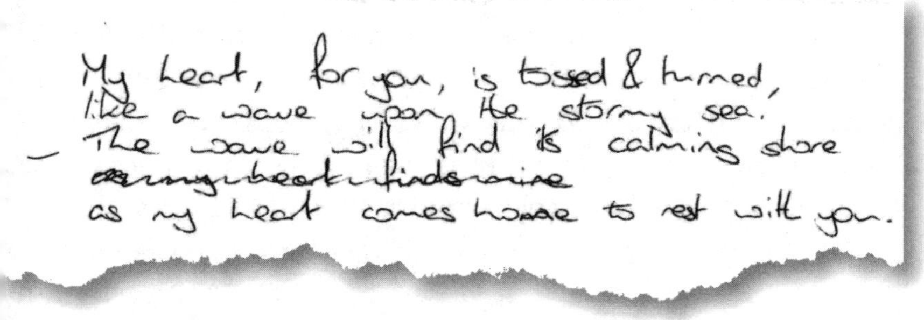

My heart, for you, is tossed & turned,
like a wave upon the stormy sea.
The wave will find its calming shore
as my heart comes home to rest with you.

My heart, for you, is tossed & turned,
like a wave upon the stormy sea.
The wave will find its calming shore
as my heart comes home to rest with you.

~~My undying love for you~~
~~and my heart felt words~~
~~is as pure as the~~
~~are~~

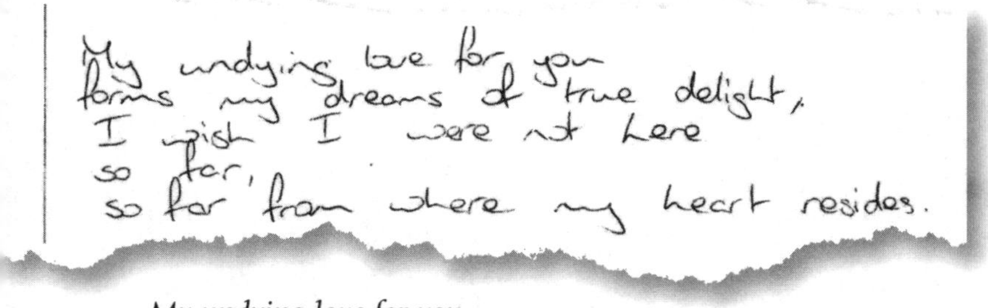

My undying love for you
forms my dreams of true delight,
I wish I were not here
so far,
so far from where my heart resides.

My undying love for you
forms my dreams of true delight,
I wish I were not here
so far,
so far from where my heart resides.

Like an albatross on the buffeting gale,
my heart is tossed and turned.

It was 1990, I was seventeen and in undying love with my girlfriend. (My undying love for her died after she went to university and things fizzled out over the two hundred miles that separated us.) These heartfelt words had to be carefully thought about – some are crossed out because they weren't quite right, weren't quite enough to convey my undying gale-tossed heartfelt adoration. I don't know why I had such a thing about storms – the weather is generally very placid where I come from.

CRUSHED SOUL

CAROLINE HOGG

I'm here, waiting.
No one else can hear my cries for mercy,
but you.
It's getting nearer,
the spirit that will trap me,
and c...

I'm here. Waiting.
No one can hear my cries for mercy
but you.
It's getting nearer,
the spirit that will trap me,
and crush my soul.
Where are you?

I can remember this poem off the top of my head. Right now. That's how deeply in love I was with it at the time. I wrote it as an extremely self-involved twelve-year-old during a trip to an artist's studio – he'd made crazy sculptures out of driftwood and one looked particularly lonely. And like its soul was being crushed, apparently. My teacher rang my mum to see if there was any huge trauma in the family. Mum was mortified.

THE BLATANT OFFSPRING

ANTONIA CORNWELL

We could not know, we, the fractured crystals
That lie at the bottom of this spiralling
ever downwards
Road of life.
We could not have known the pain we would suffer
As the wall crumbled
When you trusted your first impressions.
We could have spiralled
but we were not the common;
we were the falling ones,

April 1987

> We could not know, we, the fractured crystals
> That lie at the bottom of this spiralling
> ever downwards
> Road of life.
> We could not have known the pain we would suffer
> As the wall crumbled
> When you trusted your first impressions.
> We could have spiralled
> But we were not the common;
> We were the falling ones,
> Straight down.
> If you had believed
> That distant call that lay
> Behind the deceiving wall of blatant offspring

You would have held your place.
And now you hear once more, the voice
Of failing desperation.
It flings you to the utmost
Wall of regret
And there you crumble, you die in the dust.

I have absolutely no idea what the hell this is about. If I used to complain that 'no one understands', I'm really not surprised. What is a blatant offspring? How high can you stack them?

Are swept up trees
By falling, curling boughs,
Is secret to intruders;
and to those who might persist
The ~~tangled~~ swirling things of secrecy
would blind you in a mist.
So steer clear of the jungle,

What you see is on the edge
The regulated lines
Like trees that grow
In straightened rows
To hide the knot inside.
To struggle through the creepers
To invade the privacy
Would be hopeless, for you would not
Understand what you would see.
The jungle of the hidden mind,
Where thinking tigers prowl,
Where memories
Are swept up trees

By falling, curling boughs,
Is secret to intruders;
And to those who might persist
The swirling thongs of secrecy
Would blind you in a mist.
So steer clear of the jungle;
Beware its growling grin;
Content yourself with what you see
And go no further in.

I used to think I was really deep and fucked-up and fascinating, but I was actually a complete twat who wrote bad poetry. I am wearing a swirling thong of secrecy right now.

LUNATIC SCREAMS

DEIRDRE CONNOLLY

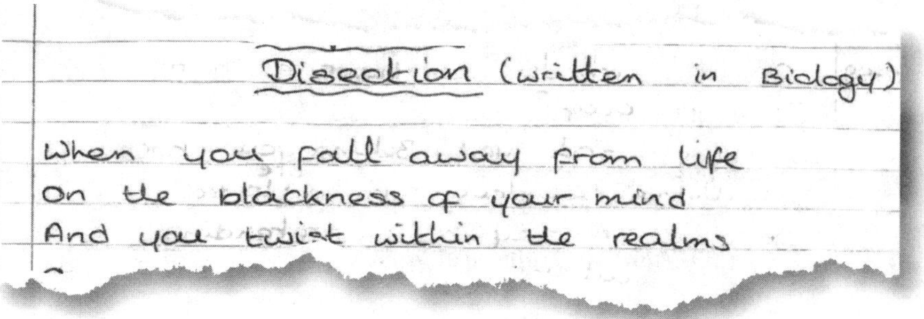

<u>Disection</u> (written in Biology)

When you fall away from life
On the blackness of your mind
And you twist within the realms

November/December 1989

Disection (written in biology)

When you fall away from life
On the blackness of your mind
And you twist within the realms
Of the unexplored awning
And you look but you see nothing.
The lunatic screams with one voice
But the crowd mumble low
In unaccounted noise
Forever you will look and
Forget what you seek
Many times beguiled by the lure of decay
Leaving – look behind you and crumble
With unparalleled fear.

This was written in Biology class, which I hated. I failed miserably in my final exams. It was 1989 and I was sixteen and bored out of my mind, so an escape into the world of the tortured teenager was divine. When I read this aloud at Dublin Cringe, my mouth was dry with mortification, but I've come to find it funny.

Stupid

I shouted at the stupid woman
Who shouted at me first
I stood upon her stupid face
And jumped upon her lumpy legs
I scratched and clawed
She screamed and lolled
Her body fat and rolling
I hated the grimace on her mouth
I hated her all whole
And hated her in bits
I killed the stupid woman
Who dared to laugh at me

I looked up and there she stood
And what did I say? 'Sorry'

Also written in Biology, about the substitute teacher (our previous teacher had mysteriously disappeared). She had just driven me into a temper and I had shouted at her in class and was sent to my Head of Year. I wasn't generally in much trouble in school and this just galled me. Looking at it now it's just as well my mam didn't find it – I reckon a trip to the guidance counsellor might have been on the cards.

Swa____ ___
So tasty and crunchy and easy to eat
Slobber all over me, then blow me dry
Iron me, starch me and then fold me away
Cover me in whipped cream, in fruity yoghurt
In sticky jam, in sticky hands
Read to me and tuck me in
Pray for me and ___ ___le me

Strange New Game

Slurp me down like a slush puppy
Suck down all my colours and leave my ice behind to melt
Swallow me whole like a honey nut loop
So tasty and crunchy and easy to eat
Slobber all over me, then blow me dry
Iron me, starch me and then fold me away
Cover me in whipped cream, in fruity yoghurt
In sticky jam, in sticky hands
Read to me and tuck me in
Pray for me and dangle me
Rafters and beams, fences and fields
Boots and blindfolds, girls and boys
Strange new game.

This was written in 1991, when I was eighteen. The influence of The Velvet Underground meets the experimentation of a teenage girl . . . It's not as embarrassing as the other poems in terms of style, but, Jaysus, talk about asking for it.

THE LIFE OF A RUBBER BAND

CHARLOTTE MITCHELL

I hope you chose me from a cabbage rather than a newspaper. Cabbage rubber bands stretch much farther, you know.

You have shown me the life of a rubber band.

I lie for short periods in a relaxed state,
My sole need and purpose being
To surround you and hold our lives together.
In happy ignorance I lie unaware of the
Arrival of your mood of indifference.
But it comes, stretching me til the
Tension threatens my whole being.
As you let go, I speed to a valley of self-pity.
Then richocet to a pinnacle of resentment.
In my effort to snap back at you
I find I have slipped unknowingly once again
To the level ground of loving you.

I hope you chose me from a cabbage rather than a newspaper.
Cabbage rubber bands stretch much further, you know.

Ah, young love – the best of times, the worst of times. I wish I could claim I was fifteen when I wrote this oh-so-deeply heartbreaking piece of drivel, but actually it was 1973 and I was a nineteen-year-old university student doing journalism and part-time creative writing (obviously very part-time). My parents' long marriage had just ended in a sudden divorce, and I was an emotional mess. I was asking the big questions. Is there really true, everlasting love out there? Can you believe anything a man tells you? Will I find someone who will respect me for my mind? Is this skirt short enough?

I fell hard for a very nice man. He was a little older than me, almost ready to graduate. I considered him to be quite intellectual. He loved books, words, poetry. He was sweet and loving and shared his innermost feelings with me. And then – he just wouldn't. The wall would come up. The wall would come down. I was totally confused. No, I was in *anguish*.

Evidently, I just had to put this anguish in writing. He needed to understand how truly horrible and frustrating it was to feel like a . . . like a . . . RUBBER BAND? I was obviously sucked into this mass murder of a metaphor and just couldn't stop. All the tension, stretching, ricocheting, snapping! He must have felt terrible. How could he do all this to a sweet girl who actually hoped she was a cabbage rubber band?

Actually, as I read this thirty years later, I don't remember giving this poem to him. Surely I would remember his reaction. Maybe I came to my senses. One can only hope.

IT'S HARD TO WRITE

JANINE ORFORD

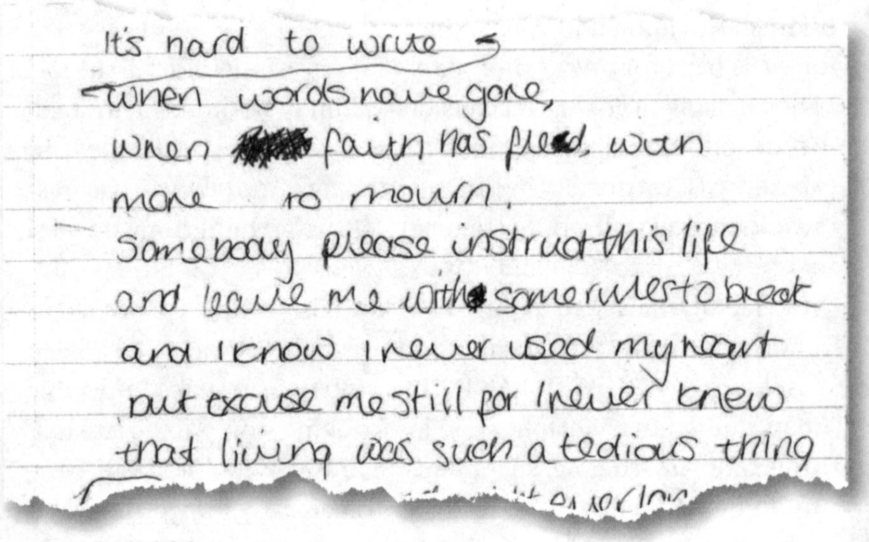

It's hard to write
when words have gone,
when faith has fled, with
more to mourn.
Somebody please instruct this life
and leave me with some rules to break
and I know I never used my heart
but excuse me still for I never knew
that living was such a tedious thing

March 2002

It's hard to write when words have gone,
when faith has fled with more to mourn.
Somebody please instruct this life
and leave me with some rules to break
and I know I never used my heart
but excuse me still for I never knew
that living was such a tedious thing

day to day and night everlong
I've seen them all! I've seen them still,
but there is something missing still and I,
I'm sure, I'm sure of what it means.
Not much I can do about it now,
just keep playing the game.

I have taken my diaries with me everywhere I've moved since I stopped living with my parents, because I've always been scared my mum or dad would read them. This is entirely justified; I had an awful diary experience once with my dad. He sent a text message to me out of the blue one day that said, 'I read your journal thingy, I really like your poems.' Firstly, why would he even tell me he had read it? And secondly, he clearly had quite a sense of humour.

I was mortified and in protest threw away the particular diary he mentioned. Of course, I made quite a ceremony of this: lots of screaming, slamming of doors and declaring that he had breached my human right to privacy. Though at the time I thought he was right; I was going to be the next Sylvia Plath, without the awful head in oven thing.

THE BOWL WITH A THOUSAND SPOONS

NICHOLAS HUGHES

Let he thrust the bowl
With a thousand spoons
And share with us the many moons
As time grows nearer

Let the distance between us
Be conquered by division
Let us not to the distance increase
But to our parts be played
And with all imagination
It will decrease.
The path be found by another
But before the honest soul
The other will cower.
Let he thrust the bowl
With a thousand spoons
And share with us the many moons
As time grows nearer
We become less and less
Be all we know is our best

It was 1991, I was fourteen and in love with a girl called Rosy, who I discovered was into Buddhism. I thought I'd try to write something that would express my deep love for her and my understanding of her beliefs. In its initial incarnation this poem was almost three sides of A4, so I spent several weeks distilling this masterpiece (as I truly believed it to be) into its current form. Having dedicated such a large amount of time and energy to this work I felt compelled to memorize it and . . . recite it to her. Please excuse me for a moment while I throw up. There, that's better. Needless to say, it did not go well. She tried her best to listen patiently, but couldn't hold in her laughter and ran away as soon as I'd finished. And, really, who can blame her.

Several years later I discovered that she had gone on to become a Buddhist nun, so at least no one else got to shag her either. I like to think that the trauma of having to listen to a spotty fourteen-year-old recite this bollocks helped her on her path to enlightenment.

I really did think this poem was going to win her heart, and if not that, at least some sort of prize for genius teenage poetry. Nearly twenty years later I'm still misunderstood and full of shit, and wondering if perhaps my prize got lost in the post. If anyone finds it, please send it to Michael O'Mara Books c/o Sarah Brown and I'm sure that she will manage to get it to me.

DREAM GIRL

AMANDA PERINO

This is an obviously first draft of what I can only describe as a rough poem, of sorts, that I composed aged fourteen.

Just wait for the twist at the end to find out who this mystery 'Dream Girl' is! You'll never guess.

> *She is apart from the others.*
> *a bubble is around ~~has~~ the*
> *other that seperates her from*
> *~~the others~~ them*
> *or is the bubble around ~~the~~*
> *~~others~~ her?*

Dream Girl

As I walk through life in my own shadows
I pass blurred visions of a girl.
Sometimes she's happy, around people she loves
But drastic changes are shown in the scene around the corner
She is apart from the others
A bubble is around the others that seperates her from them
Or is the bubble around her?
Through foggy streets I walk
Following the life of this girl
Looking forward to the next episode,
Wondering what is in store for this image of someone so familiar
As I pass each scene I feel more and more for the girl
We relate in many ways
Until I come upon the last image I can find

It is the girl
She is walking through
Foggy streets,
Chasing visions to find the destiny of herself.
Suddenly the screen goes blank and I am face to face with
        the girl
We go our seperate ways
One day I will find myself again
Until then I roam the dim lonely streets
Searching for visions
searching for myself
Visions of who I am.

PARENTS

The basic consensus is *why won't they all just die?*

NEW COAT

JO WICKHAM

[handwritten note:] we'd been going out for 2 months & he said he thought it was my birthday (as I rang up) what a pratt! Oh well, I got a Quicksilver bag today. I hate Mum. she said I can't have a coat as I still fit my old one. I'm gonna...

20 August 1997

Well, I rang Rob to see if he remembered that we'd been going out for 2 months and he said he thought it was my birthday (as I rang up) – what a pratt! Oh well, I got a Quicksilver bag today. I hate Mum. She said I can't have a coat as I still fit in my old one. I'm gonna feel like a prick if I wear a coat everyone was wearing last year. She's such a bitch. It doesn't cost <u>that</u> much and I <u>need</u> a coat. She's such a slapper. She's only doing it coz I get most things I want so she wants to say no, so I'm not spoilt. She's such a bitch. <u>And</u> I've lost my keys and she'll have an eppy if she finds out. Oh I hate her and I hate myself for losing them. God I'm pissed off – I know it's only keys but if I've lost them I'll go mad – I <u>hate</u> losing things but I do a lot. Oh I'm soo mad.

7 September 1997

I hate my mother. I was talking to her about going on holiday with N [a friend that wasn't particularly nice to me] and saying we might of fallen out then Tim [my brother] went 'no – she's a bit funny' and so that means my bitch of a mother had told him all my troubles about N. this all sounds complete shite and doesn't make sense but I can't explain it properly – God, basically it means she's been a complete cow

– I hate her. I know I don't really though, even as I write this I know I still love her but I can't help feeling angry. Argh – slapper!!

24 December 1998
It's Christmas Eve and I hate my family. I was just talking on the phone to Kaz and they all laughed at me and Dad cut me off (luckily I'd just hung up anyway). Kate was cackling and Tim was laughing like a wanker – I hate them.

An 'eppy'? Dear, oh, dear. And my mum is apparently a 'slapper' for not buying me a coat when I fit perfectly fine in my old one. Hmm, not overreacting at all there. The Christmas spirit of love and laughter with the family was utterly lost on my fifteen-year-old self.

RULES FOR PARENTING

ALICIA WOLFE

① Telephones in their rooms is a must.
Personal phone lines would be a
nice gift for a teenager. (also, extras
on the phone, like call-waiting, don't
really cost that much.)
② ... to subscribe to on...

Alicia's Rules for Parenting

1. *Telephones in their rooms is a must. Personal phone lines would be a nice gift for a teenager. (Also, extras on the phone, like call-waiting, don't really cost that much.)*

2. *Pay for them to subscribe to one to two magazines. Reading is good for them, and everyone likes to get post.*

3. *Weekends are the most important aspects of their social life. NO CURFEWS!*

4. *Support their hobbies. (If they have an abnormal obsession with James Dean, so be it.)*

5. *Let them express themselves however they want to. They can dress how they want to, use whatever language they want to, and decorate their room how they like.*

6. *Every child should have a pet, it's not fair to deprive them of one.*

7. *Let them wear makeup when they ask to. Though it may look stupid, their friends will think it's cool.*

8. *If they mention a boy's name, but don't want to talk about it further, don't make them, and don't tease them about it.*

9. *Don't give them the tatty, worn out towels. If you get new towels, they get new towels.*

10. *Rent a film they will want to watch when you have a babysitter. Babysitting is hard, and a film takes off a lot of pressure.*

11. *Buy them clothes from proper shops, don't get them crap from George at Asda.*

12. *Keep Spaghetti Hoops in the cupboard.*

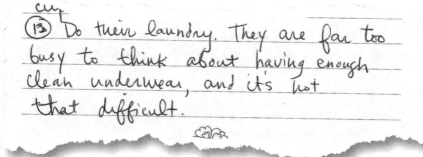

cup

⑬ Do their laundry. They are far too busy to think about having enough clean underwear, and it's not that difficult.

13. *Do their laundry. They are far too busy to think about having enough clean underwear, and it's not that difficult.*

14. *Explain puberty honestly. Don't use stupid sayings that will confuse them (the birds and the bees) and don't give them leaflets from 1952.*

15. *Let them learn the hard way, they won't believe your warnings.*

(16) Let them take turns in the front seat of the car. The front seat is a major fight starter, and it should NOT be 'oldest gets it.'

(17) If you have to buy them something expensive for school, don't make it their birthday present.

(18) Don't make them get a short haircut just because you think it looks cute. Their schoolmates will call your daughter a boy.

(19) Don't give them bad haircuts. Take them to a hairdresser and let her give your child a bad haircut. At least they can't blame you.

(20) Don't make things that you know they won't like for dinner and then tell them to eat it or go hungry (especially Chicken Kiev and sauerkraut).

(21) Don't let their siblings wake them up at 4:00 AM to clean their hair out of the shower drain.

(22) Let them decide for themselves whether or not they like other food. Some people never get to eat Chinese food because their parents don't like it.

(23) Don't follow them around, picking hairs off their back, and tucking in their tags, and generally picking at them.

(24) The remote control is family property, children have the right to change channel during the adverts.

(25) Keep more than Diet Coke in the house. Everyone else has normal Coke, and your children will be regarded as weirdos for their abnormal taste in diet.

(26) Don't make them wear horrible wooly hats with pompoms on top.

27) *Sometimes fire can be fun. Let them light bonfires sometimes.*

28) *If they are trying to breakdance and fall flat on their face and get carpet burns everywhere, don't make them go swimming the next morning. Not only will it sting, but the other children will ridicule them.*

29) *If it is cold in the house, turn on the heating. If it is hot in the house, open a window.*

I don't remember the day I started this list but it must have been in 1990, when I was the pleasant age of thirteen. However I distinctly remember the anger that inspired it. Who could forget the outrage one felt upon being denied even one single pair of Guess jeans in favour of George at Asda's version? As if I needed to be further set up for ridicule with my boy haircut, pink glasses and clear braces? I still stand by 100 per cent of this list, and my future child will be so grateful. Okay, maybe not the Spaghetti Hoops one. Or the laundry one. We may have to negotiate the remote control.

THIS IS BOOBY-TRAPPED

ANA SAMPSON

> On w...
> don't you nosey! Did
> you think I was stupid?
> This is booby trapped. I
> ...once u

20 March 1991

From now on, not going to write about stupid boys and stuff so if nosey parker family read it, it'll be ok. But, Mum/Caroline [my sister]:
I think what I think and you're spyin' anyway so you can't complain or tell me off. And if you do, that's really bad. You are not respecting my privacy at all. You're being NOSEY. I know it's tempting but just BEAT IT! Did you think I was stupid? This is booby trapped. I can tell at once if someone's read it cos I stuck a hair around it. And I have a secret way of knowing who so you're nicked! I MEAN IT TOO!

All *patently* untrue. I was thirteen at the time.

I STILL HATE MY MUM

HELENA BURTON

[handwritten note, partially legible] ...I suppose. I ...me my... I'm not a very sociable person really am I. My new motto is "strip me, whip me and screw me...

15 January 1991

I still hate my Mum. I'm not a very sociable person really am I? My new motto is 'strip me, whip me and screw me in pink jelly' but no one has so far. I think the last bit needs altering slightly.

Ana has shaved the side of her hair a little bit, but it's hardly noticeable (shame!), when you have it pointed out to you it looks really stupid though (good!). I'm getting really depressed with myself (sweaty palms, massive zit in the middle of my nose, can't hug anyone). In fact I really hate myself. So I'd better stop writing. Night night.

By the way, Lucy is a bigger slag than I am. In the slam books last year, she got 17 votes for slag of the year. I only got 16.

this -

> My Dad normally gives me
> a lift to school in the car, but
> he makes me sit in the back,
> which is really embarrasing,
> so I told him I needed a
> ... I'd rather walk

My Dad normally gives me a lift to school in the car, but he makes me sit in the back which is really embarrassing. So I told him I needed a change and I'd rather walk. Now he's going to walk with me! So I'm going to try and get up before he gets up and go without him. I don't expect Mum will let me though.

I actually had a very good family and went to a nice independent school, but you would think I was tortured by my parents from the venom I felt for them in my teenage years.

What can I say about my sixteen votes for slag of the year, except that my school friends were clearly even more innocent than me. Somehow, at that time in school, being perceived as slutty was something to aspire to, along with wearing a bra and having a perm if your mum would let you. Mine never did, which I felt really let me down in the cool stakes and probably contributed to my hating her so much. This entry clearly demonstrates my slut competitive streak though.

I think the 'screw me in pink jelly' thing may have some link with Lord Flashheart from *Blackadder*, which was popular on telly at the time, but I really can't see the connection. Whatever, that's my story and I'm sticking to it.

me to stop ...... I wasn't allowed to go to
___'s party today coz I got grounded,
my Dad thinks I'm seeing
too much of the guys + it's
affecting my schoolwork so I'm
...allowed to see them

2 March 1991

I wasn't allowed to go to Fitch's party today coz I got grounded. My Dad thinks I'm seeing too much of the guys + it's affecting my schoolwork so I'm not allowed to see them outside school. He also thinks I have been groping them! I told him I didn't know what it meant, but he dragged it out of me in the end, which made it worse coz I lied to him.

By the way, I haven't touched a penis since I was 9 years old. I think my Dad has been reading my diary, or else how else does he know so much about my life while Mum is still so naive. So fuck off Dad, please, this diary is for my reference not your nosiness.

Dad has got the flu. His temperature is 110. I hope he dies.

Well, what can I say about this entry? If I remember rightly, there may have been some rather minor 'behind the bike sheds' snogging going on, which my dad took to be more serious than it was. How on earth did I think he would believe that a fourteen-year-old didn't know what groping was, though? I clearly had no idea about anyone else in the world beyond my own self-obsessed head. And evidently parents are stupid, everyone knows that. I seemed to wish they were dead quite a lot from the ages of thirteen to eighteen. Mostly because they wouldn't let me wear denim, or would try to make me tidy my room.

To this day I have no idea whose penis I saw when I was nine. I think that might have been a bit of wishful thinking, or possibly the boy next door showed me in exchange for first go on the rope slide.

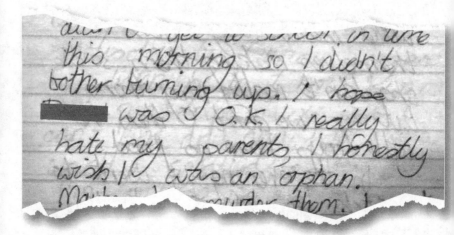

Mum and I did manage to get a school skirt, some clarinet reeds, some jazz clarinet music and an airtex blouse for school. I didn't get to school in time this morning so I didn't bother turning up. I hope Ishmail was O.K. I really hate my parents, I honestly wish I was an orphan. Maybe I'll murder them. I want some ice cream.

I love that this page contains a detailed list of all the mundane things we bought from the shop and then right at the bottom, as an afterthought, I say that I didn't bother going to school, wished I was an orphan and was considering murder. (That's only marginally more important than wanting an ice cream apparently.)

I don't remember ever bunking off school when I was younger (too scared) so this may have been a bit of wishful thinking on my part, although I don't know who I thought would read my diary that wasn't likely to ground me. There's a tantalizing possibility that I might have played hooky and had all kinds of adventures, but I'll never know because I can't remember, and all my journal contains is a shopping list and pages and pages on how much I hate my mum.

I KNOW SHE DOESN'T LOVE ME

JANINE ORFORD

on things.
I had started to write a letter to Mum,
in which I stressed how I hated liars and
so in turn I hated her.

30 December 2001

9.02pm – *Today has been a particularly bad day. Still, it doesn't help
to dwell on things.*[1] *I had started to write a letter to Mum, in which
I stressed how I hated liars, and so in turn I hated her.*[2] *She doesn't
want me around. Lately I've matured. I realise that telling people what
you wish causes anger, and if I was to die tomorrow I'd want everyone
to know I don't hate anyone.*[3]

*At the moment I'm continuing to read Villette. I think I shall buy
all the books written by the Bronte's and by Jane Austen – though I
don't find the latter too appealing. I think I should also buy poems by
Dylan Thomas and Robert Frost. This summer I want to read War
and Peace.*

[1] Though I'm sure I'll give it a good go.
[2] How lovely of me.
[3] Always thinking of other people.

I'm not sure why I was so precise with the diary times – perhaps it was in case I was ever called up as a suspect of a crime. I'd be able to quickly respond, 'But no, sir, that could not have been me, for as you will see here at 9.02 p.m. on the night in question I was far too busy brooding.'

In the seven years since, I have not read *War and Peace*.

LOVE! ~~ALL~~ I want really. I don't think I've ever had that. Mum can <u>say</u> it tillshe is blue in the face but I <u>know</u> she doesn't love me. She knows that deep down.

28 April 2002
LOVE! <u>All</u> I want really. I don't think I've ever had that. Mum can <u>say</u> it till she is blue in the face but I <u>know</u> she doesn't love me. She knows that deep down.

Although the pain of life was a recurring theme in my diary, the pain of living with my parents in particular was something I touched on once or twice. If they did happen to read those particular excerpts, they only had themselves to blame.

GOOSE FAT

ANNA MACONOCHIE

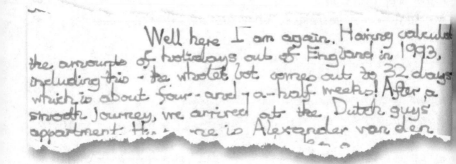

Saturday 29 May 1993, 8.03 a.m.

*Well here I am again. Having calculated the amounts of holidays out
of England in 1993, including this – the whole lot comes out to 32
days which is about four-and-a-half weeks! After a smooth journey, we
arrived at the Dutch guy's appartment. His name is Alexander van
den Boogert. His building overlooks a canal surrounded by plants,
people and buildings. It is an attractive and varied view.*

*It is a business getting into his actual home. We are situated high
up. We firstly had to locate numbers 36-37 which was a small
archway, walk along a short passageway and climb ten of the steepest
stairs I have ever seen. We finally reached his front door.*

*Olivia and I unpacked onto a chair each and underneath it in
the living-room because this is not a bedroom. We share the living-
room as our bedroom.*

*Olivia was talking about a friend of her 10-year-old brother Johnny's
called Bertie Snowball. Can you imagine such a name? What if he has to
go to a business meeting. Olivia is my oldest friend now – since we were
eight. She is thirteen now like me and next year is going to boarding school
in the heart of the country. All three of them will be at boarding school.
What is the point of having kids? At least she will be nearly fourteen.*

Sunday 30 May 1993, 9.45 p.m.

Today was an eventful day. Breakfast was now acquired and I set up the table. We had apples, grapefruits (which we thought were oranges), tea, coffee, and various juices. I put out anything I suspected could be eaten with toast. The bread was toasted by my mother. We sat down. Daddy decided that this guy who lives here is a little weird due to the style of his flat. Little things like no washing-up liquid, only one bin, an incredibly varied style in art and furniture.

We sat happily down to breakfast. I brought over a cardboard packet of something like sugar. My Dad had nearly tipped a spoonful into his coffee when he said 'This does not look like sugar...' It was indeed baking powder. I thought I was spreading jam onto my toast when I realised it was pickle. The olives and raisins that we had been eating earlier were off by 1991. But the final climax was when I brought a very big jar of honey over. Olivia opened it with some difficulty, loaded her knife and then my father advised her to test it just in case. It looked a bit weird – too pale. She took a tiny bit and then said 'Yuk, this is not honey.' It was GOOSE FAT. Who would need goose fat? 'He must be a cannibal,' said my father. How true, I thought. That explains our strange little incidents. He even had an electric slicer for some mysterious reason. Well, not mysterious any longer.

I was thirteen when I wrote my first travel diary, and this section, from a family trip to Amsterdam with a school friend in tow, comes from that. The idea was to keep a written record of anywhere I went out of London and during 1993 that ranged from Norfolk to the American West. I don't know why I started the diary – I think I was inspired by a friend of my mother's who was quite a committed 'travel diarist'. I enjoy looking back over it now because so many details seem banal but at the time it mattered to me to get everything down. You start from one place – the new location, the different food, what your friend is wearing, but you end up with so much more, namely a portrait of your family and friendships and ultimately a portrait of yourself that is rather different from the self that thinks it is writing the diary . . .

I'M DYING

NINA GOTUA

Sunday 28 November 1993

Dear diary,
My mother is driving me nuts! When she is angry, she looks like a
monkey.

> My mother and I had another awful fight
> last night. She said I can't watch TV. She
> should never have said it, never have done it,
> She doesn't know how much it hurts. I w...

Sunday 5 December 1993

Dear diary,
My mother and I had another awful fight last night. She said I can't
watch TV. She should never have said it, never have done it, she doesn't
know how much it hurts. I need everyone I love around me but they're
not and I feel so alone. Gone are the happy days, they are replaced by
shadows so dark and large, so frightening so cold, that they block out
everything happy that happens to me. Mother says she understands, but in
my heart I know that she doesn't, and maybe that's what hurts the most.
Not being understood. If she understood, she would have comforted me,
not yelled at me! Another resentment, and if it goes on like this, I'll be
brought to a point of not caring, when I don't care about anything that
happens to me. Sometimes I feel that way. Often I begin to wonder
what is there so great about my childhood, my adolescence. Nobody
understands, nobody understands, nobody understands, maybe that's
what makes it so sad, not being understood.

believe they're making me go again to Yugoslav school! ▮▮▮▮ is going to teach me math, to fill up my 'holes'. Hah! I know why the rest of the children think of her as a

Sunday 12 December 1993

I'm dying. I mean it. I'm loaded with homework and I have a stupid biology test coming up tomorrow. I had a chemistry test on Thursday and it killed me. I studied so much that I got a headache (and an attack of hysteria). That night I kept having nightmares about chemistry, shouting something about carbon dioxide (I told you I studied far too much!)

I want to kill my Mom. Yesterday I went to see a friend, Marina, and Marina's mom is a math teacher in a Yugoslav school. I went there last year, it was hell. Sometimes my mom is such a moron, such a monster, witch sadist, she abuses her child mentally and is in a way just as bad as Mr Martin (my math teacher) – they both have greasy hair and sometimes drive me nuts, although mom is not six feet tall. My mom and Marina's mom are a pack of witches. Mom (Witch 1), Marina's mom (Witch 2)! I can't believe they're making me go again to Yugoslav school! Marina's mom is going to teach me math, to fill up my 'holes'. Hah! I know why the rest of the children think of her as a witch. Learn from all your experiences.

Moral: Never let your parents stay together long enough to exchange opinions on their kids, because if they do, they are likely to find a 'reasonable' solution, that the children don't like. My mom is making me have an extra French lesson, all I need!

Moral: Never let your mother talk to a French Teacher. Witch 3 = Frenchteacher. Also Witch 3 convinced my mom that I shouldn't read any books but French. What a fuck! What a monster! What a moron! She should unite with Sadam Hussein. What a . . . (there isn't a word bad enough to describe her). She can destroy a nation faster than both Sadam and Slobodan Milosevic (Yugoslavian monster president).

I can only imagine what a treasure I was to have around the house during my teens. This level of hysteria and rage is, I'm afraid to say, a fairly representative example. A sense of proportion is not something I was troubled by at this age – Saddam Hussein, Slobodan Milosevic and my French teacher . . . a trio of evil.

LOVE & SEX

At fifteen they rarely occur separately, much less together (and the same goes at thirty, let's face it). However, this pesky fact doesn't stop anyone from trying it on, least of all hormone-addled teenagers with no experience and nothing to lose.

IN LUV

MAUREEN LEVY

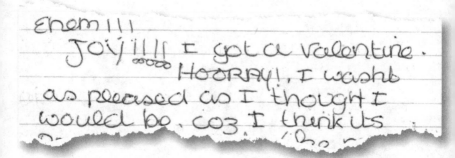

12 February 1974

Ehem!!! Joy!!!! I got a valentine. HOORAY! I wasn't as pleased as I thought I would be cos I think it's from Philip Katz and hes revolting or Alan Cantor (yugh!).

I LUV TREVOR.

Roz got a HUGE VALENTINE from Bernard. It was about 2 feet high and really soppy. It said 'kisses spread diseases – lets start an epidemic' Listened to the Luxy top 30.

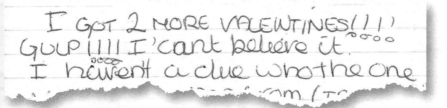

13 February 1974

School! another Bloody history lecture. Came home.

I got 2 more VALENTINES!!!! GULP!!!! I cant believe it. I haven't got a clue who the one yesterday was from (TREVOR?) (TOO MUCH TO WISH FOR???) But today were definitely Philip Katz + Alan Cantor.[1]

I'm awfully pleased and greedy PG [please God] *one more pleeeze!!!*

14 February 1974

Bloody school unfortunately.

HOORAY! Super Day! Mitched all the [history] *lecture.[2] I've got 3 valentines. One's from 'Pussy', but I dunno about the others. TREVOR (PG) I got more than anyone else. They were so shocked when I told 'em that they accuse me of sending 'em to myself. They really think I'm awful.*

To hell with everyone! 'Cept Trevor

[1] Turns out they were from Mum and Dad . . . my worst fears confirmed!
[2] I have no recollection of 'mitching' (bunking off) anything . . . beats me.

23 February 1974

Katherine and I put our plan for Roz into action. David Green said he'd dance with her as soon as the right moment came. Anyway to cut along story short he tried to get off with her but she didn't respond so that was that.

I don't think Richard likes Kath. My crush on Trevor is gone – we're still friends, but that's it. I now have a crush on David Jameson. He's 16. GULP!!! I had 2 slow dances with him. The first was medium. I thought he was going to kiss me. (Stupid expectations.) I trembled + froze. When it was over, I shivered for bout 15 minutes. V. embarrassing.[3] P.S. He uses Brut.[4]

---

[3] Every single moment of my teenage years was embarrassing.

[4] The height of sophistication for a teenage boy. How I miss the fragrant waftings of Brut mixed with really rank BO.

I'm in LUV. It was hell in school today, I was teased like mad. it was fun actually. David rang me up (Sharon had been saying a

11 March 1974

I'm in LUV. It was hell in school today. I was teased like mad, it was fun actually. David rang me up. (Sharon had been saying about him getting off with Gillian and everyone was calling him a baby snatcher) (well, shes 2 weeks older 'n me.) He said what he meant was hed never get off with anyone who acted twelve again (compliment??) My knee's were knocking for about half an hour after it then he rang back t'say Hi again.

Listened to radio Luxembourg.

I'm going with him I reaeey like him.

12 March 1974

YAY!! I'm going with him. I really like him. Failed Irish and scraped through History.

1 May 1975
I love Trevor[5]

5 May 1975
I love Richard

25 May 1975
I love Julian

13 June 1975
I love Ciaran Daly

23 June 1975
I love Richard [Was this the same Richard, or a different one?]

7 July 1975
I love Ronny

August 1975
I love Marc

October 15 1975
I love David

March 1976
I love Ian

I was thirteen at the beginning of these entries (hence the reference to 'baby-snatching' by older man David) and was always falling truly, madly and deeply in love. Nowadays they would be called 'crushes', but in the 1970s 'LUV' ruled! It meant never having to say sorry and it never lasted longer than two or three days. Alas, I still have a new crush every five minutes . . .

[5] Ah, Trevor. I should have stuck with him; he's a multimillionaire now. But he kissed with this mouth closed . . . yeugh.

SOUTH OF THE BELLY BUTTON

ANDY FOSTER

The year is 1992. John Major is seeking re-election as prime minister. Boutros Boutros-Ghali has just taken over at the UN. U2 have just released *Achtung Baby*. Meanwhile in South London, a young boy aged fifteen, our protagonist, is trapped at an all-boys school struggling with religion, politics, and desperately wanting to meet girls. As we join him he has decided to try and find God by joining the local church youth group. His mum has told him that there might be girls there . . .

Saturday 15 February [church youth group weekend away]
Gradually I began to fall to Gemma whose hair looked 1960s and amazing. Gemma is definitely not a flirter and I felt a bit uneasy when I wanted to cuddle her and so I didn't at all.

Everyone gave everyone big hugs when saying goodbye and I now feel nothing for Amanda yet a lot for Gemma as she is mentally mature even she'll only be 15 in September.

Sunday 23 February [after church youth club]
There was no push away when I put my arm around her. But ahhhh I didn't get a kiss off Gemma at the end because I was on bicycle and couldn't get off in time before she'd disappeared.

Duncan knows someone who has to take 9 Es before even getting a buzz – he must be really fucked. If I ever take an E (if I can afford it) it will certainly just be a one off even I really enjoy it as I don't want to screw up my life – the same goes for tripping but I don't think I will ever do dope once as smoking anything does nothing for me.

The Phil Collins album Face Value is excellent if I'm a bit bored or depressed.

Friday 28 February [after church youth group]
We walked back to Gemma's & chatted for over an hour about anything and everything. The only reason I haven't asked her out if because I wouldn't know where to take her as I don't know her friends and she doesn't know mine. But I didn't eventually get my goodbye hug.

Sunday 1 March
I walked Gemma back to her house as we could both talk for ages to each other about anything and she's really attractive. Then her Dad opened the door and invited me in which I did of course. He knew me as he said 'Hello Andy' but I'm not sure how? I said goodbye on the doorstep with her dad watching which will hopefully not happen next week. PLEASE, PLEASE, PLEASE!!

Sunday 22 March
I didn't hug Gemma but we were getting on and she suggested we went out on Friday. That's when it's going to happen I'm positive.

Friday 29 March
After school I met with Gemma and we went to see 'Prince of Tides' [Barbra Streisand film] *still seem scared to make advances on Gemma and over the whole afternoon and only hugged her once on the train platform – I was far too slow and stupid.*

Thursday 16 April [playing a bassoon solo in the local youth orchestra]
Help! This is the day of my concert. Soloist Andy playing third movement of Mozart Bassoon concerto.
I wanted Gemma to be there so I

could play the final notes whilst staring into her eyes as if I had performed it all just for her. But she didn't come so no such luck.

Saturday 18 April
After going to see my cousin Roger it was interesting to find out from him about not taking a lot of Es as you never get anything like your first buzz. You must always keep doing drugs in proportion with the rest of your life as its just about enjoying yourself which you can get from drink and friends.

Wednesday 13 May
I've now been totally open with Gemma. My love for Gemma will seriously diminish if I haven't got off with her in the next week. She's getting lots of flak at school with people writing Gemma 4 Andy all over the board.

Wednesday 20 May
Gemma and I seemed to ignore each other on Sunday evening so I suppose its all finished since I could never kiss her since she had never done it before. I would still have liked to go out with her if she was a bit more grown up. She's got the looks I'll give her that.

My stomach is seriously bulging and it has just got to disappear very quickly and I've also got to build up my biceps and then I'll have absolutely no fear in taking off my T-shirt and showing all.

Friday 19 June
I think I tried some spliff for the first time on Saturday although I didn't really inhale I didn't feel anything.

Well I finally got off with Gemma. Big Deal! I didn't even feel that pleased. I feel some romance with Gemma now. Yet with future older girlfriends I feel I would be worried about how far to go for my sake not theirs. I would be scared to let them go anywhere south of the bellybutton yet I wouldn't be afraid to do the same to them.

THIRTEEN

JANINE ORFORD

Jesus! Alex is a lesbian? Seems like I am the only girl who isn't attractive to anyone over the age of 13! It doesn't make me pathetic,

7 June 2002

Jesus! Alex is a lesbian? Seems like I am the only girl who isn't attractive to anyone over the age of 13! It doesn't make me pathetic, just a loser in terms of the teenage social norm.

I was sixteen and had never had a boyfriend for longer than two weeks. I am quite relieved that my shock was not with the fact that she was a lesbian, but more the fact that it meant that this was now another person in a relationship, and I still didn't have a boyfriend. The only 'offers' I'd had at that point were from boys all aged thirteen or younger. I was utterly depressed by this.

Inserted in my diary at this point was a love spell given to me by my friend Donna. In a Spanish lesson I'd said to her something along the lines of, 'God! I really love XXX, I wish he'd notice me, I wish there was some sort of spell to make him love me.' And she supplied me with the following love spell:

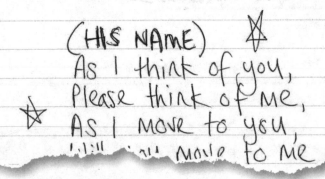

(HIS NAME)
As I think of you,
Please think of me,
As I move to you,
Will you move to me,
As I call your name,
I send mine to you.
Let us be together,
Together in love,
And it harm none,
So be it.
(Say three times every night)

JOEL

NICOLE BOGLE-DIXON

> You'll never believe it I like some guy at
> work! (yeah me the boy hater) His name is
> Joel, he's chinese and 18 oh there's just
> one thing - he's taken. Trust me the first

8 August 2000

You'll never believe it I like some guy at work! (yeah me the boy hater)
His name is Joel, he's Chinese and 18 oh there's just one thing – he's
taken. Trust me the first boy I actually like and he's taken! Tanya
reckons I should still try and go there but I'm not like that, but it
makes me so sad. I often think of him even when I see a Chinese
person or see Chinese food I daydream about what are life together
would be like. I imagine myself carefree and in love – yep that's
definitely a daydream. See that's why I HATE being 17.

> I saw Joel today he was on the late shift
> he didn't seem his cheery self usually
> he would be gliding around the shop

14 August 2000

I saw Joel today he was on the late shift he didn't seem his cheery self
usually he would be gliding around the shop floor making jokes but
today he was different. Turns out he had an argument with his

girlfriend – what a bitch, Joel's an angel how dare she upset him all day I just wanted to say 'forget her Joel you can do better' but I knew that would be wrong plus the fact that he was upset made me think he must really care about her – bitch.

Anyway the girlfriend came to New Look to see Joel – the bitch couldn't even wait until he got off work she had to bring his business to the shop floor! I would never do that. She was in tears and rambling shit, then wait for it Joel also starts crying – erm yeah he was crying they had a huge episode in the middle of New Look.

That's when I realised Joel's the complete opposite of what I thought he was (as a boyfriend) to be honest he's a bit of a fucking wimp – sobbing and crying over what I could only make out as utter bullshit. I think I lossed my mind for a minute there, what the hell did I see in him? I may be only 17 but I know I'm looking for a man not crybaby Joel.

Forget him – plus new guy Steven just hit my radar, he's looking good these days.

'I often think of him even when I see a Chinese person or see Chinese food.' Yes, I actually thought that, and then wrote it down.

A DILEMMA INDEED

LINDSAY DAVIES

The year I turned fourteen, 1986, was a big one for me. Previously my diary had focused mainly on mind-numbingly detailed accounts of my school day, and the bewilderingly complex changing allegiances of my female friendships. The opposite sex was barely mentioned and my only major crushes were confined to such unattainable sex gods as David Bowie and, er, Michael J. Fox (as I wrote in my diary, 'He's so gorgeous I have to take steroids every time I see him,' and no, I don't know what that meant either).

However, it was over the course of this momentous year that I first properly noticed the boys around me and, presumably as a result of the same pragmatism born of desperation, they began to notice me back. The turning point was when my mum finally caved in and allowed me to have a perm – costing a not inconsiderable £14.50 – which, apparently, made me 'look like Whitney Houston' (if Whitney Houston was white, had braces and used blue biro for eyeliner). With this bold move came a newfound confidence in my sexual powers: as I solemnly noted on 28 January that year, 'My face is getting better-looking by the second.' (It wasn't.)

From that point on I changed almost overnight from a studious and shy child to what can only be described as an unholy slapper. Frankly, reading this now, I can only gape in horrified admiration when I consider the speed at which I slashed and burned my way through the various spotty youths who had the misfortune to cross my path. The following typically eventful week charts the demise of a four-week-long 'relationship' with a glamorous older (i.e. fifteen-year-old) boy from a nearby school, Darren. I'm sure he'd be delighted to know it took me two whole days to get over him. Still, that was considerably longer than for most of my other conquests.

Thursday 18 September
Terrible on way home. Went down to Redhill and Darren saw me, ran up to me really happily, and I told him I didn't want to see him again. His face really fell and I felt so horrible. I really hated myself. Got home and I cried my eyes out. Really regret it. David rang up and we mucked about. Hair looked nice today.

Friday 19 Still really upset about Darren. keep thinking of him & everything we did together – wish I'd kept him. I'd be at his house now if I had. Oh God why is it I want him now? Life is damn cruel sometimes. Borrow a noth

Friday 19 September
Still really upset about Darren. Keep thinking of him and everything we did together – wish I'd kept him. I'd be at his house now if I had. Oh God why is it I want him now? Life is damn cruel sometimes.

Saturday 20 September
Caz came round this morning then we went down to Redhill. Gorgeous bloke down there. Went into Redhill Sports and bought 3 pingpong balls so we could go and eye up the blokes there. Bought stiletto poster. Then went to Reigate, and Andy B came out of work and he sat with me and Caz. He ended up with his arms round me. We then walked home (Caz being an extreme gooseberry) with his arm still round me. Put my arm round him too. Then when he had to go back I kissed him. Properly that is. Feel a bit guilty as I only chucked Darren two days ago. Don't intend on going out with Andy permanently. He is sweet though. What the hell am I going to do about him? A dilemma indeed. Put poster up.

Sunday 21 September

I keep thinking about how strange it was that I got off with Andy yesterday. It happened so smoothly I hardly even noticed it. Weird eh? God though, it was good to kiss someone again, be one half of a pair. I didn't realize how much I needed that until I chucked Darren.

Monday 22 September

Didn't see Andy! Not once! We were avoiding each other all day but now I realize I actually did want to see him! Decided I fancy Jason amongst others. Embarrassing in English – did poem about Mark in secret then at the end he goes 'Did you do your poem on me eh Lindsay?' I was so embarrassed – he must have known! Went to Redhill after school, chatted to Tim and . . . DAVID! For ages. God I hate him, he's so lovely. Saw Darren briefly too but he ran off.

Tuesday 23 September

Saw Andy but only grinned at him (made a prick of moi but still). Mark flirted round me like mad today. In Maths flirted like MAD with Neil and Mark but got moved and told off by Simpson who yet again held my cleverness against me. At lunchtime pissed about with Tim and all the other blokes. BUT – scandalous News Of The Day! APPARENTLY Jason FANCIES ME! I freaked out when I heard.

Walked home with him – had a great time. He's so CUTE!
Hope it's true.

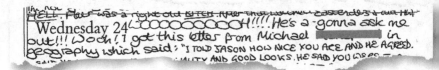

Wednesday 24 September
WOOOOOOOH!!!! He's a-gonna ask me out!!! Wooh! I got this
letter from Michael in geography which said: 'I TOLD JASON HOW
NICE YOU ARE AND HE AGREED. I SAID YOU HAD A LOVELY
PERSONALITY AND GOOD LOOKS. HE SAID YOU WERE JUST
RIGHT AND HAD A LOVELY BODY AS WELL.[1] HE LIKES YOU
A LOT BUT ISN'T THE SORT TO JUMP IN AND TELL YOU SO.
I KNOW YOU LIKE HIM AND HE DOES AS WELL. FROM
MICHAEL.' WOOOOH! So I sent Michael a note back saying if
Jason asked me out I'd say yes.

Thursday 25 September
WOOOH! At break (1st) Caz shoved me into the canteen with Helen
and we stood around feeling self-conscious until Jason (mm!) came
over and ASKED ME OUT! (high pitched scream). God I'm in love.
Bored Helen stupid going on about it. Sat with him in everything and
he was so nice. I'm in love I'm in love I'm in love love LOVE!!
JASON!! He's so gorgeous! So happy now I could die.

Friday 26 September
Went round with Jason all breaks except lunch but he sat with me
then. Walked to and from school with me. God he's so nice to me and

---

[1] I do wonder whether Michael was deploying a sophisticated sense of irony at
this point, as a later diary entry reveals that after I eventually snogged him too
(but of course), he told Mark who told Caz who told me, 'He'd like to go out
with you, but he won't coz you haven't got any boobs.' Which was harsh, if
sadly accurate.

I'm so mean to him! Like on way home I was holding hands with him and I saw . . . Darren! And I was so mean I let go of Jason's hand – I felt so guilty afterwards. Jason and I have to get over the small problem of him speaking to me otherwise it's going to get well embarrassing.

Saturday 27 September
Went down to Redhill with Caz this morning. Looked really stylish – black cap with really great outfit. Really dreading roller disco but went anyway. Met Jason inside – awkward at first. Caz went round with Lisa a lot so I was LEFT! But it was OK cos we actually kissed properly! Still reckon it was his first though. Chatted to Andy lots, saw David and Darren but didn't speak much. To Darren not at all. Really confused about seeing him again, all the old feelings. Jason seems so young.

breakfast, dinner and tea. Just my look.
Horrible day today really. You see, I've decided I'm going to chuck Jason but I have to do it slowly for his sake ... to ... + wat ched. The ...

Sunday 28 September
Horrible day today really. You see, I've decided I'm going to chuck Jason but I have to do it slowly for his sake. Went to Caz's and watched 'The Thing' with her – absolutely brilliant. Chatted and got very depressed coz of Jason. Also can't stop thinking about Darren. Why is it I always want what I haven't got? Really miss Darren. Even Andy.

I love that I decided to dump Jason because he seemed 'so young'. Whereas I, as you can see, was the height of sophisticated maturity.

ALL DOLLED UP

MATT MUIR

It's Thursday night and they're all dolled up
Time to go out for a fight or a fuck
To leave on the prowl, to unfurl their wings
For these are a few of their favourite things
The lager, the women, it's all about pride
When you're out with the lads then there's nowhere to hide
The looking, the leering, the scent of the prey
The piss-drunk numb gropings, the mind-numbed next day
'Cause you don't know her name, just the taste of her lips
And the one thing that counts is the size of her tits
For when the next morning you wake up in bed
The only real things are the pains in your head
And the girl lying next to you's only a number
Scratch up another one, pillaged and plundered
But she doesn't care, 'cos she got her shag
No matter if everyone thinks she's a slag
Hell, all of her mates will have done the same thing
And the bloke will be gone by the time the clock rings
So I stand and stare as I watch them go out
The men with their swagger, the girls with their pout
And as they pass me they'll think 'sullen twat'
As I'm left there wondering 'why can't I be like that?'

I lived in Swindon until I was fifteen. I never even got close to getting any. When I moved to Oxford, I hoped things would immediately change – they didn't. This poem was written in 1996 while I bitterly watched other people get ready to go out on what I presumed was a night of unbridled sexual excess. It is the primal scream of the lonely rage of a sixteen-year-old virgin. It is rubbish.

ANDREW'S GIRLFRIEND

ANTONIA CORNWELL

Dear Somebody whoever thou art:
Hello darling. You know something? I'm
DEFINITELY in ♥ lerrv again... it's with...
Andrew! I've mildly fancied him for
some time and now I know I fancy him
quite a lot... fancy Ken a bit too just

Friday 8 April 1988

Bed

Dear Somebody whoever thou art:
Hello darling. You know something? I'm DEFINITELY in lerrv again.
. . it's with . . . Andrew! I've mildly fancied him for some time and
now I know I fancy him quite a lot. I fancy Ken a bit too but not as
much, I don't think. I hope ONE of them at LEAST likes me or I'll be
mega-disappointed.

Saturday 9 April 1988

Dear Somebody,
ANDREW ASKED ME OUT!!

My GOD I don't believe it! I'm so HAPPY! I could just SCREAM for joy!

Oh my GOD . . . I don't believe it – he fancies me, oh THANK YOU GOD . . . this has never happened before, being asked out by someone I'm desperately in love with! Just wait until the others hear . . . I'm so HAPPY . . .

He said Monday night, Drummonds, 8 pm. Drummonds is a bit yuppie, but . . . oh he's ASKED me . . .

Andrew's girlfriend. I've managed to fill that prestigious post of Andrew's girlfriend. ME!!

The good thing is I know he must be asking me out not just for my looks but my personality too, because I talked to him a lot yesterday . . .

My dreams are true! He fancies me! It didn't seem POSSIBLE! I've got him ALL TO MYSELF!

I wonder what we'll talk about on Monday. Oh God I hope I get off with him. I may not, but I know that at least he'll kiss me. I've kissed him once before, at Rania's party. I wonder if he fancied me then?

Andrew . . . oh GOD I've got to calm down. It's like being thirteen all over again! But I'm so deeply in love, it's impossible!

Dear Somebody,
All I can think about is Andrew. I'm deeply in love with the idea of going out with him; I hope tomorrow night will be as good as I imagine it to be

Sunday 10 April 1988

My Radiator

Dear Somebody,

All I can think about is Andrew. I'm deeply in love with the idea of going out with him; I hope tomorrow night will be as good as I imagine it to be. Tomorrow! It seems impossible, somehow. And the good thing is, I'll see him after that, too, because I'm going out with him. I'd be heartbroken, I think, if he didn't fancy me . . . but I think most of this simpering has been brought about by the prospect of him fancying me too. If he was going out with someone else, I reckon I'd hate him for it and that would put me off him a lot. As it is, completely the reverse has happened and I'm in a complete spin. I now know what they're talking about in slushy books, songs and short stories because I'm beginning to sound like one myself!

Oh I do hope tomorrow works out well. I'm making myself remember what to do and what not to . . . no shyness or inferiority complexes because that would put him off me. No, I'm going to be outgoing, confident and as interested in him as possible because according to How To Win Friends and Influence People, and personal experience, that's how to go about a successful relationship. Andrew gets put off by girls with inferiority complexes. I'm assuming that he likes my personality, and every time I've been with him it's been at a party, so I've been chatty and lively and really outgoing. So I'll keep that up but I won't pretend to be what I'm not, if you see what I mean. I'll see if I can get involved with organising his party, because that's something that interests him and he'd probably like it if I showed a sincere interest in it too.

I'm SO in love! I won't write any more before it gets too slush-infested!

24 April 1988

My bedroom

Dear Somebody,
I MUST tell you about last night! We went to 2 awful pubs in
Richmond. Andrew's sort of into astrology, like I guess a lot of people
are. He sat up the night before last and did his and my solar charts.
All the character descriptions on mine are 100% accurate, and he and
I have a LOT in common! For example: we both fear rejection and
isolation, are looking for a long-lasting relationship, and lots of other
things I can't remember.

We left Richmond at 10ish and went to my house. No one was
around so we spent at least an hour getting off on the sofa. Andrew
developed wandering hands syndrome – I didn't think he had it in
him! He took off his glasses about halfway through - he looks really
different without them.

On my bike ride today, I started having second thoughts about
last night. I didn't mind Andrew touching me up at the time, but
today I was thinking that somehow I prefer to think of him as more of
a caring person than 'just after one thing' as blokes usually are.

I'll leave you now – I'm absolutely knackered.

Four hours later

Dear Somebody,
How can I ever explain or describe what I feel for Andrew? I am just
so in love, so hypnotised by him, that I can't think about anything else
but him. The wonderful thing is he loves me too: he did my star chart
before his – which shows he must have a sincere interest in me as well
as being in love with me. I just know we're going to last a long time
even though today is only our 2-week anniversary.

2 May 1988

My bedroom

Dear Somebody,
There's nothing worse than missing someone, is there? Yes, I know I'm
boring but it IS Andrew again. I haven't seen him today.
*   I saw a programme about the Rolling Stones and their Hyde Park*
concert for Brian Jones. Mick Jagger looked really – beautiful, is the
best word for him, really pretty and sensual and all those things he's
supposed to be, and now I've decided I want to be beautiful too, and
I'm going to grow my hair long (which I've been doing since winter
1986 anyway). I'll make myself a few summer dresses – must have
flowers on – and I'm determined to stay with Andrew for as long
as I can – all through the summer – so I can be pretty for him
especially. I LOVE looking nice for him. He's so sweet and caring and
understanding and unpretentious and he's just so lovely and so pretty.

1 March 1989

My bedroom

Dear Somebody,
I'm so mixed up. I don't know whether I love Andrew any more. He's
not as nice to me as Simon is. I feel tied down. I'm 17, feel 47 and I
want to die. I really do think I prefer Simon. What can I do?

7 April 1989

Bedroom

Dear Somebody,
The Big Break has occurred – several weeks ago in fact, but I know
now that it's definite. Andrew and I are no more: I'm going out with
Simon now! I feel really groovy – I've just read my letter to you of
exactly a year ago and I was in the same euphoric mood then, going
on about keeping fit and looking great. It must be the time of year; I've
been worrying about keeping fit again over the last 2 days or so –
haven't done anything about it though as the weather's been foul for a
week – before that it was sunny and it is now, too. But that's boring.
I met 'Jimmy' last night (that's a joke between me and Elizabeth:
she's met Ken's 'Jimmy' (on Tuesday) so I set about meeting Simon's
last night in the car – and I gave him a b.j. Didn't get in until 2.45
this morning, mind you that's been quite a regular occurrence lately.
The latest time Simon left was after Monday night, when Tash had a
party – S. left my house at 4.a.m. on Tuesday morning! – it's so
incredible. I think he's a real turn-on; he really wants to screw me and
vice versa; he promises it won't hurt. We're going to do it next week
one day because I'm on the curse at the moment and anyway he'll
have the house to himself next week when his mum goes back to work.

I've got about 1½ weeks of holiday left – my first driving lesson's on April 17th! Cool. I go back on the 18th – God help me. I think I'm going to fail A levels, I can't hack the workload.

Well – I must go and wash my hair.

These are the diary entries that follow my first 'serious' relationship when I was sixteen and seventeen. His name was Andrew, he was well-spoken and mild-mannered and he had dark hair and glasses, and we were terribly in love, until I got bored and fancied someone else. I left him for Simon, who lived in a tower block in Isleworth and wore lots of stonewash denim, and who used to put Pink Floyd on the stereo before snogging me. We never did Do It, though.

20 NASTY THINGS ABOUT MEN

1) Ruddles County – what – burps?
2) Fruit machines – not so bad What?
3) Football
4) Television *
5) Testicles
6) willies (limp) Yes
7) congealed smeg under foreskins NASTY! ✓
8) smeg in general
9) those who aim smeg into your tummy button!
10) grunting
11) *

20 NASTY THINGS ABOUT MEN

1	Ruddles County
2	Fruit machines
3	Football
4	Television
5	Testicles
6	Willies (limp)
7	Congealed smeg under foreskins
8	Smeg in general
9	Those who aim smeg into your tummy buttons!
10	Grunting
11	Smelly armpits/feet
12	Wearing socks in bed
13	Condoms
14	Farting
15	Dangleberries
16	Stubble scratching on your face (for too long)
17	Dribble
18	Men who flop down exhausted after an orgasm + leave you sitting there completely frustrated

19	*Whips + chains*
20	*MEN!*
21	*Scratching in bed*
22	*Reading on the toilet*
23	*Flirting*
24	*Button-fly jeans*
25	*Y FRONTS!!!*
26	*No loopaper in the loo*
27	*Annoyingly cheap belts that WON'T undo!*
28	*Men who cry on the phone*

List of '20 Nasty Things About Men' that had twenty-eight items on it. It was the summer of 1990 and I was eighteen: clearly I had not ever slept with anyone old enough to be a real man because 'Talking about mortgages' and 'Not putting away power tools' aren't in there. What makes me cringe about this are the little reminders, like 'Ruddles County', of the horrible boys I did things with. Brrrr.

TWENTY

HELENA BURTON

20 May 1991

People I fancy: Mike Jones (I got off with him a few weeks ago when we were at the Mauretania – this is a really cool club we go to, as it has good bands playing there and is generally a VERY good scene).

> *youth leader at Red Cross ('Aaagh!') but I can't help it. He's 20, he listen to rave, drives a ford capri and wears shell suits but he's driving me crazy. I don't know why. Anyway that*

David Stone (Red Cross) – he's now our youth leader at Red Cross (aagh!) but I can't help it. He's 20, listens to rave, drives a ford Capri and wears shell suits but he's driving me crazy. Anyway, that couldn't work anyway, coz he's five years older than me, my parents don't approve and although he got off with me at the middle of this year, I don't think he fancies me now so I'll just have to grow out of it.

In my diaries there are pages and pages of lists of boys who I fancied, changing about every week and based on very little apart from how popular I thought they were.

The Mauretania seemed incredibly cool at the time, but in retrospect it was just a pub where they served Southern Comfort and lemonade to fourteen-year-olds and I was always picked up outside by my dad at ten thirty. It was closed down shortly afterwards for under-age drinking.

I remember David Stone, he was a butcher in the supermarket and was twenty. Therefore, despite the shell suits and rave music, he was hot stuff to a fourteen-year-old. We ate chips on the bonnet of his car once and I thought that was so rad.

SERIOUSLY CONSIDERING IT

ZAN MCQUADE

28 December 1993

Tonight I saw Andrew again. He's really tall and really nice and really willing. He said 'i'd love to get off with you, but i can't. i really would.' the problem is that he's got a girlfriend (20, Guernsey) and he might just want me for sex. He told Jo that he could give me his address and his parents are out during the day and i seriously considered it. i seriously am considering it. i've bought condoms and everything. but the more i think about it the more horrible it gets. there are some really great factors to it: he's a wonderful first time, he's English, he's thin, he's cute (enough about him), i could go home a new woman and be able to tell my friends, I would feel more mature. But there are also a lot of bad factors as well: AIDS, pregnancy, the parents, I could hemmorage like Sylvia Plath, his girlfriend, walking funny, pain, his largeness (he's tall at least). The lists (both) could go on. I really don't think that i'll do it, but it's very weird how seriously i'm considering it.

i wonder if my parents would be more upset if i came home without my hair or without my virginity.

I was seventeen years old, spending two weeks in a tiny town in the middle of England over the Christmas holidays, and apparently intent upon kissing as many British boys as I could get my virginal American paws on. As soon as I met a few older boys, however, it became apparent that kissing might not be enough . . .

It's amazing how worked up we get over the prospect of losing our virginity. At the slightest thought of it, suddenly every single catastrophic possibility comes clambering up into our brains and we envision ourselves as the heroine of some horror film, clawing our faces with our fingers. It wasn't as simple as deciding if he was the right guy for me; it was all of those awful things that could happen as a result of sex that seemed to occupy my thoughts. Because every time you have sex you are bound to have something horrible happen to you. Aren't those the rules?

If I'm completely honest, though, what really makes me squirm the most when reading this is the realization that he was probably just being polite and he didn't even want to have sex with me at all.

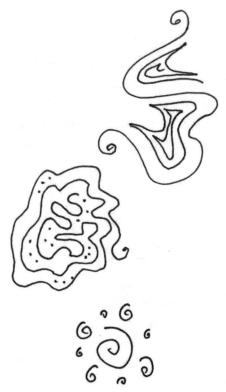

RYAN

KAZ HARRISON

July 1997

I think I'm turning into a sad cow. I still fancy Ryan. It's July. I have fancied him since September . . . does the word obsession come into this? Or WHAT?

OH MY GAWD. Hot gossip off the press – Becky fancies IAIN!!! She confessed this morning!! Sad cow! (well I suppose I did fancy him). But now I fancy Ryan Craig Seed. We get 82% on the 'loves' scale. Becky and Iain only get 64.

Almost the end of school (hooray!). Jo and Lindsey have found love (lucky girls). YEP in Jem and Tom. And (shock horror) Jo has forgotten how many times she's got off with Tom!!!

I wish I could be over Ryan.

October 1997

Right, I have just got back from Germany (Germany . . . sigh!) and found out that someone has been spreading really awful rumours about me. The rumour got passed round to Katherine and now she's not speaking to me. It's really hurting me. I bet it was Mary. Anyway, I found out that the rumour was that I was a . . . BITCH.

Oh, I heart Ryan Seed. He has just got a new bag and looks really sexy.

21 June 1998

Just re-read my diary. oh my God, I can't believe a whole year ago I fancied Ryan. I was over him in March. I fancied him for 2 years. I'm glad I'm over him.

Tuesday 7 September 1999

Oh and I love Ryan Seed.

Saturday 13 November 1999
Ryan told me I have the sexiest hair in year 11. Oh I love him.

Saturday 27 November 1999
I want Ryan. I love him so much

Saturday 5 February 2000
I kissed Ryan Seed last night (at Hys) to 'think twice' by Celine D. I must remember that song. Oh, it was so slow, yet so fast and passionate. He was very good. We kissed for 40 minutes and he was definitely hard!!!!!

These entries span from 1997, when I was thirteen, to 2000, and show how I basically fancied the SAME guy for the whole of secondary school.

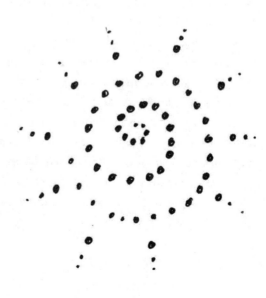

DUMPED

LUCIE KEETON

That means I'm gonna have to do loads of jobs! cos dad'll just sit around reading the paper I saw Stacey in the shop this morning she was going to Brockholes. she looked terrible (she said she got stoned - this early?)

Sunday 18 June 1995

Father's Day

It's that day.

That means I'm gonna have to do loads of jobs! Cos Dad'll just sit around reading the paper!

I saw Stacey in the shop this morning, she was going to Brockholes. She looked terrible (she said she got stoned – this early?)

This thing with Andy, I'm sure he's gonna finish it on Monday. Because, well . . . we're supposed to be 'going together' and we've not even seen each other over the weekend. I should have rung him, I know, but he could have rung me. He said before that he hates it when it gets boring, well it is pretty boring, every day, it's like, we're in the common room, and he or I go over to the other one, and we just talk and stuff, we never walk round much, its pretty much like a habit.

I've decided if I can help it, I'm not letting Andy go – I've just been thinking about Bude, and well, it was really good then so why can't it be now?

Tuesday 20 June 1995

I've had a really shit day. Andy finished with me. I knew he going to,

150

cos I didn't see him yesterday and I didn't see him morning break. But about half way through lunch he came in and said 'do you wanna come for a walk' – I was already pissed off cos he's ignored me once today and all the people I was sat with knew I was.

We went up to the common room and then we were almost at his form room and he said 'I just wanna talk to you' – then I knew what he was gonna say. I told him I did and he said he really likes me and he would want to go with me again but not at school.

I was in a foul mood for the rest of the afternoon. Everyone was being really nice though. We had D+C and I couldn't stop looking at him. I kept catching his eye and I could feel him looking at me sometimes.

It's gonna be such a shit week now I'll be seeing him everywhere. But I don't hate Andy and I wish I did cos it'd make it easier, I knew one of us would end it soon but I don't believe it now its happened.

P.S. I found out Helen fancies Andy . . . so do I . . . I feel so empty . . .

P.P.S. We're going to Pizza Hut tonight, me, Sarah, Claire, Heidi and Emma.

I was fifteen. I was dealing with the excitement (and apparent boredom) of my first boyfriend . . . I seem to display the beginnings of schizophrenic tendencies as I state that I 'feel so empty' in one sentence, immediately following that up by talking about pizza.

LIKE JORDAN FROM NEW KIDS ON THE BLOCK

NOREEN KHAN

6 December 1993

Now I am 13 and today we organized a fete and I have just found out that we raised £50, half for the Old Folks' Party, and half to the WWF.

Samah's aunty got married and at the wedding me and Nadia saw a gorgeous boy with lovely green eyes. I think he liked me because he kept looking our way, but it could of been Nadia. There was another boy I liked. He was a lot like Jordan from New Kids on the Block. The boy with the green eyes was very, very good looking and Nadia got jealous because I had the courage to ask him the time and Nadia was mad.

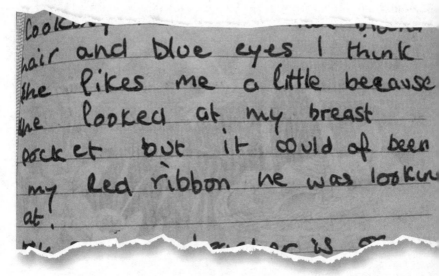

My Art teacher is good looking. He has nice blonde hair and blue eyes. I think he likes me a little because he looked at my breast pocket,

but it could have been my red ribbon he was looking at.

My science teacher is alright, I think he keeps touching me, because once he tried to touch my eyes and the second time he, or something, brushed against my leg. Now I have to stop and go and watch Desmond's.

Every time I read this extract it makes me shudder . . . what a load of mind-numbing rambles. Having a diary meant so much to me at the time; having a secret book, with a secret location. I thought I was the bee's knees at school because I had a diary with a lock on it.

I guess at thirteen you begin to be more aware of yourself and your surroundings, and in my case, develop an active imagination. I do remember that day very well; it was my aunt's wedding day and I was wearing this over-the-top, handmade shalwar kameez, which was a fruitcake of sparkles and colours. To be honest, that's probably why the green-eyed boy was looking our way. I was wearing the sartorial equivalent of a road accident you can't help staring at.

6 April 1984

Dear Stacy (foxy),

Even though I haven't known you that long, I already love you more than anything in the whole wide world. I hope you love me the same way. I was just thinking of a few poems to write down and here they are:

> *Roses are red,*
> *Violets are blue,*
> *The grade we're in doesn't matter*
> *Because I will always still love you.*

> *I would love you very much*
> *If you were Roman or if you were Dutch.*
> *You are terrific either way and I would make love to*
> *you any day*
> *(just kidding)*

They are not the best, but I tried. No offence on that last poem. I thought it was pretty cool.

*   You will be getting my picture soon. I wish I could be with you*

every minute of my life. I think of you all the time. You are so
beautiful. I had to say that.

I was afraid you were going to say no when I asked you to go with
me. I am never going to break up with you. I almost forgot to tell you,
if anybody (a boy) bugs you just tell me because I will kick his ass in.

I hate to say it but I have to go, bye bye.

Love always,

Mike

I LOVE YOU LOTS!

13 April 1984

Dear Stacy (foxy),
Hi! How are you? I haven't been better since I asked you to go. I love
you more than anything in the whole world.

I wish you were with me at the movie tonight so that we could
hold onto each other during the scary parts (most of the movie).

I am about to fall asleep, it is 11:48pm. I wish you were here to fall asleep with me. All I think about now is kissing and frenching you. I hope my thoughts come true at the skating rink this Sunday. Do you hope my thought come true Sunday.

I don't know why I am talking about Sunday because you won't get this letter until Monday or Tuesday.

I am going to ask you a few questions, OK. How far do you want to go with me? Why? Where? When. Tell me the answers the next time we talk to each other.

I LOVE YOU!

I had to say that. Our song (Hello, by Lionel Ritchie) is playing on the radio right now. I just thought of a poem, here it is:

> I would french you any way
> In a car,
> On a train,
> In the kitchen,
> On a broom,
> But most of all I would like to french you in my room.

Did you like that poem? I hate to say it but I am about to fall asleep. I better say, GOOD-BYE!

Love always,
Mike

P.S. I love you!

Sorry, so sloppy W/B (write back)

These letters were given to me by my first boyfriend when I was eleven. Don't let his hormone-charged missives fool you: we never so much as hugged. And also don't let the nickname 'Foxy' fool you either: you can see from the photo that I was anything but.

SELF-EXPRESSION

Before you own your own flat or car, you have to have some vehicle with which to showcase your intense personality. You spend hours cultivating and creating the thing that just perfectly sums you up: hairstyles, comic strips, songs, *Smash Hits* magazine collages.

We can't all be poets, thank God.

WEEKLY POLLYPAPER

POLLY HAYES

This is the 1988 centrefold of the *Weekly Pollypaper* that I issued during my school summer holiday when I was fourteen, because I was sad and had no friends. This is issue one. There were no more issues.

Check out the amazing twist in the short story; it's enough to blow you away. This does not make me cringe at all, it is brilliant and I am now a successful short story writer and astrologer. (This is not true.)

A Short Story by Pollz

He dialled, and put the phone reciever to his ear. He took a long drag of his cigarette as he listened to the rings, then exhaled deeply and sharply as there was a sudden reply on the other end.
"5261. Hell female voice, but not Kathleen'

A Short Story By Pollz

He dialled, and put the phone receiver to his ear. He took a long drag of his cigarette as he listened to the rings, then exhaled deeply and sharply as there was a sudden reply on the other end.

'5261. Hello?' A female voice, but not Kathleen's.

'Erm, hello – is Kath there?' He tapped his cigarette irritably on the side of the ashtray. He hadn't expected it to go like this.

'I'll just get her for you.' The tone of voice became sterner at the sound of his deep male voice.

'Thanks.' God, why had Kath's mother had to answer? It could've gone so much more smoothly if the phone had been answered by those sweet dulcet tones …

been answered by ....

His dream was interrupted by the bossy voice again.

"She's just coming." As soon as she left the phone,
Roy yelled "Fuck off you brittle old hag!" into the
receiver. Just then, a lovely young voice sprang onto the
phone.

"Hello? Is that Roy?" It was Kath.

His dream was interrupted by the bossy voice again.

'She's just coming.' As soon as she left the phone, Roy yelled 'Fuck off you brittle old hag!' into the receiver. Just then, a lovely young voice sprang onto the phone.

'Hello? Is that Roy?' It was Kath.

'Hello Kath? Yup, it's me.' He scuffed around for the bit of paper that he'd prepared. On it was written what he had to say.

'Oh, hi. What did you want?' God, where the hell's that paper? Ah! Found it! He unfolded it.

'Yup, it's about the reservation for tonight. Table for two, please.'

'OK. Table … for … two … – hang on, I'm just writing it down – near … do you want one near the window or the kitchen?'

'Window please.' He hesitated. Should he change his mind? No.

'OK. Window table for two.'

'OK. Bye.' Making reservations at Kath's Café wasn't the same as it had used to be …

FINIS.

"Ok. Window table for two."
"Ok. Bye." Making reservations at Kath's Café wasn't
the same as it had used to be.....

FINIS.

YOUR STARS

Aries
You should be doing OK for the moment but watch out for coming troubles in romance OK?

Taurus
Financially you're doing well but if you've got the money, don't splash out. Think first.

Gemini
If you're having troubles at the moment, be yourself – don't be a poser – and they'll pass!

Cancer
You seem to be dividing your time well at the moment – but if you get fed up, contact an old mate. You could have lots of fun fun fun!

Leo
If you've been going through a lot of stress lately, find something to do – even a holiday sports course is better than nothing.

Virgo
Keep your virginity while you've got it, if you've got it, for luv is in the air...

Libra
Don't put yourself through any unnecessary pain at the moment – keep cool + friendly + it'll all blow over.

Scorpio
Havin' a luvly time? WATCH OUT! Money matters are lurking!!

Gemini.
    If you're having
troubles at the moment,
be yourself—don't be a
poser—and they'll pass!

Sagittarius
        If you're bored,
liven yourself up! Write a
few letters? The effect will
be astounding!

Cap—

Sagittarius
If you're bored, liven yourself up! Write a few letters? The effect will be astounding!

Capricorn
Don't be pissed off. You still have friends so use them before it's too late or you really will be pissed off!

Aquarius
Ha ha ha! Isn't life fun? Free as a birdy! But don't take anything for granted 'cos everything'll go topsy-turvy if you do.

Pisces
God you look pissed off. Liven yourself up you boring old fart! Don't forget that you may be losing your friends through depression – you may be pissing them off!

WHAT I LIKE

ANA SAMPSON

I tend to put together lists of disparate things that are floating my boat at any one time, and these make entertaining but often baffling reading. The first is from 1992 (aged fourteen) and the second is from 1994 (aged sixteen).

WHAT I LIKE:
Alan
Snowballs
Cleansing pads
Jenga
Mexican Night
Frogs
Prince/Nirvana [Yeah, because they are interchangeable, really.]
Lost passports [?]
Bombers [I am assuming this means bomber jackets and not, you know, actual bombers.]
Phil's slippers [No idea . . .]
Prawns
Chris' mauve jeans [Really?]
Stubble
Now That's What I Call Music Vol. 23

WHAT I LIKE:
The Divine Hammer [This was the name, originally of a
Breeders song, I gave my army bag . . . I don't know why]
Baileys
Claire
Balls
My blue jeans
Blind Melon
House parties
The word 'knobhead'
Tequila
Pure Black Levis
White Musk
Mellow mix tape
My DM Boots
HAVING A BEAUTIFUL LIFE [This must have been
during an 'up' mood swing!]

12 April 1993
*Ok, in years to come, I'll laugh at this but I do honestly think I'm
growing up right now . . . My bedroom is becoming my own at last –
dark-coloured, vivid bed and curtains, mirror, pics on the door, Lenny
[Kravitz] on the walls, pictures everywhere, hippy beads on the handle,
tapes in piles on the chest of drawers . . .*

This diary entry was written when I was fifteen. Obviously, I was on
first name terms with Mr Kravitz. It doesn't sound that radical, but
for a long time I wasn't allowed to put up pictures, or newspaper
cuttings about Kurt Cobain, or to cut out words from old copies of
Smash Hits that 'spoke' to me – things like 'MYSTIFY' . . .

WHO IS YOUR IDOL?

LYDIA MARKOFF

These are the things that were pasted onto the cover of an address book I made for myself in 1992, the summer before I started college.

FRONT:
'Another reason to be Winona Rider'
[I was totally obsessed with her. I even signed myself 'The Blonde Winona' in people's yearbooks. Jesus.]

Panel from a 1987 comic titled Love Adventure:

> Two girls lounging on a bedroom floor.

Panel intro: *There were these very popular bushes in our neighbourhood where practically everyone on the planet got their first kiss. Me and Deena said we got ours there too by somebody's cousin from Idaho but it was a lie. We had never kissed no one.*

Speech balloon: *No one's ever gonna kiss us, man. And nobody*

even believes us about that guy from Idaho either. Who'd ever kiss a guy from Idaho?
Reply: *At least we're not sluts.*
Rebuttal: *So?*

[If you weren't a cheerleader and pretty in that conventional way in my high school, you got no play from the dudes. This is pretty much how I felt about the whole thing, despite having had dates with three guys by then. Also, the thing about the sluts? A majorly self-righteous virgin, I comforted myself, post-being-dumped, by deciding that the New Girlfriend was in fact a raging slut. She wasn't, at all.]

'WHO IS YOUR IDOL?'
[Um, what? No clue here.]

Photo of a pair of cowboy boots on a sandy beach
[I was saying something along the lines of, 'I might be going to school back East, but my heart will always be in Texas! Honest! And I am going to wear my black cowboy boots all over Manhattan for the next two years to prove it, then . . . um, never live there again.']

'GIVEITAWAY'
[Testament to my brief and unfortunate Red Hot Chili Peppers infatuation.]

'He would never date your best friend . . . would he?'
[Got dumped by long-time friend who had become more. He then took up with my best friend's younger sister. See the last part of the comic panel.]

'Mike Edwards is my future husband'
[The singer from Jesus Jones. I liked 'em tall, skinny, dark-haired and musiciany.]

Photo of Ann Richards

[She was the Governor of Texas at the time. She reminded me of my grandmother; strong and funny and down-to-earth, but powerful and shit. I imagined I might be Governor some day. Yeaaaah, no.]

Screenshot of the dwarf from *Twin Peaks*, with the words '*She's filled with secrets*' below.

[*Twin Peaks* was my biggest obsession at the time. I dressed like Audrey Horne, I wanted to be all dangerous and damaged and weird like everyone on the show, I wanted to live in the misty Pacific Northwest, I drank coffee like they were going to stop making it tomorrow, I haunted whatever diners I could find, I decided to name my future dog – a black Labrador, who is to this day still only hypothetical – Agent Cooper, I called my friend Cindy during every commercial break to scream about what we just saw. I'm surprised I didn't cover the entire notebook in this stuff.]

BACK:

'*I'm too pale*'

[If you are a schoolgirl in Texas, this is what you always think. By the time you are in your thirties and have sun-damaged skin with age spots, it is too late to tell yourself what an idiot you are.]

Quotation from 'Summertime Rolls' by Jane's Addiction:
'MY GIRLFRIEND DON'T WEAR NO SHOES. HER NOSE IS PAINTED PEPPER
SUNLIGHT. SHE LOVES ME. I MEAN IT SERIOUS AS SERIOUS CAN BE.'
[I only knew two Jane's Addiction songs, but I bought all their CDs
and acted like I totally got them, because I thought it
was indie and cool. This quote I liked because . . . I
have freckles. And this seemed to make it OK.]

'Depeche Mode'
[Mode. You gotta get into Mode if you want to be taken seriously
by the alternative types. Funny thing is, they really are awesome
and I love the shit out of them now – I was just putting a toe in, at
this point. I probably couldn't have picked a single one of them
out of a line-up, even if the other people were Bruce Springsteen,
Michael Jackson and my brother.]

Small photo of Matt Dillon.
[Because, hell yeah, Matt Dillon.]

A speech balloon cut from a comic – probably the same one as on
the front cover – that says: 'Auuggh! She's so sleazy!!'
[Again, see the last line of explanation about the comic panel.]

A fifties photo of a young woman in a cap and gown, holding a
diploma, overlaid with the words 'No money for college'.
[Columbia cost $25,000 a year at that time. My dad made nowhere
near that, at least not on the books. I spent my entire high school
career hustling for stuff that would get me scholarships. It worked,
but what a fucking grind – and when it was all over, and I got in,
I never did anything above and beyond ever again – burnout city.]

Excerpt of broken-hearted emo teen poetry:

> *Speaking to you*
> *I feel gaps that before were bridges*

And silences that before were words
Afraid to bring up dried emotions
I think by talking about things
You revive them
Like running water over a sponge
It's not enough for us to say so much
But still circle around what should be said.

[Is it really necessary to explain that this was all about the ex-boyfriend? I didn't write it, but I sure as hell could've. We 'stayed friends', which in practice meant he would speak to me in public, and I put on what was probably the world's worst game face – even going so far as to agree to a triple date with him and the new girlfriend, another couple, and me and his best friend – while carrying on my obsessive bullshit, as if no one knew I was doing it. There may or may not have been drive-bys at the new girlfriend's house, is all I'm saying.]

INSIDE BACK COVER:
A profile of the Capricorn personality, which includes the line *'Has beautiful eyes tinged with sadness and wisdom.'*
[What teenage girl wouldn't fall for being flattered like this? It was everything I totally thought or wanted to think about myself at the time.]

2086
JOSH GALLAWAY

My friend Scott and I would write and draw comics, and each of us would credit the other as 'editor' on what we made. I created this one in 1987, when I was thirteen. It's called *2086*, and is a blatant rip-off of *Thunderbirds 2086*, if anyone remembers it.

Scott and I had a comic company called Spiral, and we marked everything 'For Mature Readers'; we did have the self-awareness to laugh that it was written by immature readers, so that's something.

These things took me forever to make, and I would take my drawing board and pencils everywhere, trying to get away so I could get to work. I really feel like these comics are what I should show people in job interviews to prove that I am driven, but we all know you can't do that.

You may notice a tendency of every single character to fly off the handle at any moment and scream and bitch profanely at the top of their lungs. This is because they are all thirteen years old, you must remember. It's a tough time. Your teachers are stupid, your mom and dad treat you like a little kid, the guys in eighth grade call you names on the bus, and then you've got a galactic war to fight. Can no one understand?

Here are a few selected excerpts . . .

Panels 1–2: So we find our hero John Oscoff, serial bad speller, on board the *Alpha*. He's doing something awesome. What could it be? What do you think it is?

He's reading *Playboy*, for the articles. In his red jumpsuit, on his day off, with hair done. My main influence was Manga, I swear, but he's got a bit of a Mötley Crüe look to him, unfortunately. The eighties, they are a fluid that soaks into everything – his other combat boots have neon laces, I'm sure of it.

Panels 3–5: And now he's pissed off when someone knocks. He's thirteen, so you have to expect it. But then he's happy because it's Scott. I mean Dilan Beta.

As a child, admit it, you thought this was how adults acted. Actually, maybe I know some who do, but I try to avoid them. These dudes have a big-screen TV, you can tell. (The bad proportion on Beta's head makes me cringe more than anything else. I knew better than that.)

Panels 1–2: So, the two comrades take off without authorization, and some damn teacher or mom or asshole from eighth grade on the bus challenges them. This calls for shooting something. That's better. (You're thirteen, remember?)

Panel 3: God damn idiot . . . I know how you feel. He's dead now, don't worry.

Panels 1–3: Maybe the baddie, Dr Starstan Stranto is more level-headed than the good guys. Turkey? Boar? Assholes!

Panel 4: 'WHAT THE FUCK IS GOING ON HERE???!!!!' You can tell this is the bad guy. He doesn't pussyfoot around; if you called him a God damn idiot you'd be combing broken glass out of your ass for the rest of your life.

Panels 5–8: Oh the violence! The horrors of life! We humans are but ghosts trapped in these bloody things!

174

So, Oscoff and Beta showed up, the shit has been in the fan for fifteen minutes, and all he can think to himself is, SHIT. Shit. Shit, I have to recopy a page of my homework, shit, the dudes in eighth grade hit me again, shit, my arm is gone. Shit!

P.S. In the next issue, Stranto totally kicks all their asses and escapes. And a planet gets destroyed! Seriously. Buy the next issue. See you then!

PYROMANIAC

AMANDA HOUK-COPLEY

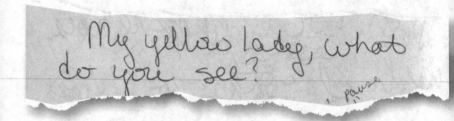

My yellow lady, what do you see? (pause)

A song (slow)

My yellow lady, what do you see?
My yellow lady is (pause) ('is' optional) looking at me.

(Chorus)
Yellow lady what (stop short)
do you see? (Not like a question) (Each word sung slowly)
Ask the yellow lady
what it means (sung low and slowly)

Yellow lady, hold hands
with these hands (a little faster then slow again)
Yellow lady I can take
you to new lands
Without you all my clouds
drop low (sung low deep)

Come with me and will (build crescendo)
make a rainbow (go lower but end in a high note)
With our souls
so fresh sh sh sh (into background fade)
The colours tear off
our flesh sh sh sh (fade)

They get to the <u>real</u> (long 3) meaning (slow)
Yellow lady, tell me what I'm feeling (very slow) (stretch really long)

Music gets louder, goes back to chorus and repeats over and over again 'what does it mean' in sort of a chaos, cries out the words in a torment type of feeling, running out of time feeling, then fade away after singer says it the last time in a cry of despair.

(Inspiration – a trivial pursuit game)

Amanda Houk

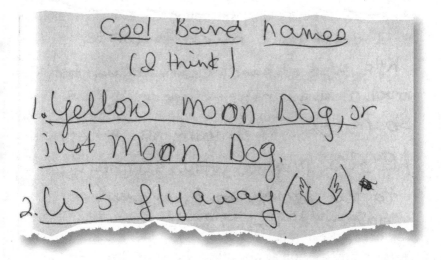

Cool Band Names

(I think)

1. *Yellow Moon Dog, or just Moon Dog.*
2. *W's fly away*
3. *No more Books to Read*
4. *Electric Chair*
5. *Shang-ri-la*

6.   Pyromaniacs (sing yellow lady (fire))
7.   Tattoos ('the' optional)
8.   Bite your tongue
9.   What are looking at (?)
10. Raven (optional – Hair)
11. Lost our lease
12. Flea market
13. Running out of (words) (music) (freedom) (choices) (money) (ink) (time) (power) (optional)

While I had (and still have) absolutely no musical ability whatsoever, I went through many stages of fancying myself quite the composer. It was 1993, I was around fifteen and, like many my age, had become obsessed with fire. A regular pyromaniac, I wrote a tribute song to my new love: flame. Even though I had no idea what I was 'arranging', I took it all very seriously (as you can see from the detailed, if incomprehensible, notes). I think I faked through it pretty well and was ready to start coaching my band. Even worse than rereading my 'music' is that I remember practising the song in my room and writing and rewriting my notes, like a frantic teenaged Beethoven, studying her patchouli incense for inspiration. How could I get my lyrics to drift like smoke?

All this led to a list of 'cool' band names. My imaginary band (number six, Pyromaniacs, of course) would begin prepping for 'Yellow Lady' as soon as possible. I would also like to point out that there was a glimmer of my future in marketing as I was already sketching out a logo for band (number two, 'W's fly away').

PERFECTING MY LOOK

ANTONIA CORNWELL

(Left to right)

1. 1982, aged ten: Not quite a teenager. This is me at ten with my friend Tamsin. I think I lightly pencilled some eyebrows onto the photo around 1987, when I was fifteen and didn't want to be seen aged ten with no eyebrows.

2. 1983, aged eleven: First official ID photo. I thought I should look serious.

3. 1984, aged twelve: First official secondary-school portrait. I longed to be a punk, and deluded myself I looked like one with short hair. At weekends I would put my hair in lots of tiny elastic bands sprouting from all over my head, and wear a studded choker with my M&S pullover and pastel trousers.

4. 1984, aged twelve: First year of senior school. I was considered one of the very trendiest people in our year by my peers, purely because I read *Smash Hits* and knew who was in which band, as well as the lyrics to their songs. In this year, I wore boiler suits to school, which were terribly 'in' and worn by lots of people's embarrassing mothers. I had one in khaki and another in bubble-

gum pink. Oh, and I had braces, and went and got my ears pierced without asking permission.

I was so cool.

(Left to right)

1. 1984, aged thirteen: In the autumn term of my second year of school, when I wore tube skirts and granddad shirts, plus long cardigans and chunky bangles. I had a second hole pierced in my left ear, which was considered terribly outré. Only the bold followed suit. I got my first boyfriend this year. His name was Rory and he was six foot eight. I was four foot ten. We never kissed. We went to see *Cocoon* at Richmond Odeon, during which we had a silent battle as he tried to get his hand into my pants and I tried to keep it out. We walked home along the Thames towpath and sometimes he'd say something and I'd have to say, 'What?' from two feet below. There was no second date.

2. 1985, aged thirteen: Spring, after the most disastrous haircut of my life. I had a free voucher for Vidal Sassoon and thought, what can go wrong? This, is the answer. I looked like the bastard spawn of a quick knee-trembler between a lavatory brush and a Cabbage Patch doll. Oh, and I wore red, black and white baseball boots, plus black and white tartan-print cotton baggy trousers that were too long for me and that I consequently rolled up so I had doughnuts round my ankles, as one of the local boys described it.

3. 1986, aged fourteen: Growing out the haircut.

4. 1986, aged fourteen: Still growing out the haircut. By this stage I had acquired a long black overcoat and black baseball boots. I

wore black magic marker on my eyelids because, unlike eyeliner, it lasted all day and didn't smudge. It didn't catch on. During the spring holidays I got a second hole pierced in my right ear and a THIRD in my left. My mother said, 'You will stop now, won't you, darling?' I stopped.

(Left to right)

1. 1987, aged fifteen: Here I am having tired of growing out the haircut and lopped it short. My hair was likened to that of the lead singer of Swing Out Sister, and this pleased me. My friend Rose thought my nose looked like a knob, as she illustrated on the photo.

2. 1987, aged fifteen: Spring. This is when I wore teeny miniskirts, clumpy boots, an Aran jumper and a denim jacket, plus black tights that always had holes in. Also, brass curtain rings for earrings and black rubber Hoover bands on my wrists. I had just bought the new Communards album, and listened to it constantly. I fancied the specky one out of the Communards until I saw him one day at Hammersmith tube station and he looked really pasty and spotty.

3. 1987, aged sixteen: This is me at my sexiest ever. I put my hair in plaits the night before to achieve this coveted demi-wave look. Also, the photographer made us say 'Cornflakes', the idea being to catch us on the 'Flakes' and thus smiling, but I was unfortunate enough to be caught on the 'fl' and look like a demi-waved rabbit instead.

4. 1989, aged seventeen: Summer, and I am successfully pulling off the *Love Story* look of flowing hair, a tan, and come-hither

snuggly knitwear. That's what I thought I was doing until the booth spat out this photo.

(Left to right)

1. 1989, aged eighteen: Autumn term. Here I am trying to look foxy for the school photographer. He will not catch me saying 'fl' this year. Instead I assume a dreamy, ethereal attitude, maintaining it even as my friends press their faces to the little glass window in the door and frantically take the piss.

2. 1990, aged eighteen: You know when you get dressed, or you buy a new piece of clothing, and chuck your hair all over to one side, and you think it's going to make you look a certain way? And then you have your photo taken in a photo booth and you actually look like this? That happened to me a lot. QED.

3. 1991, aged nineteen: This was the photo I had taken for my university applications. I wore a lot of paisley at this point in my life, and lots of tie-dye. And waistcoats. And frilly-hemmed petticoat dresses. My father laughed at me and said I looked like an extra from *Dr Zhivago*.

4. 1991, aged nineteen: Nearly out of the woods and almost, almost human.

MAXINE'S TAXI

JO WICKHAM

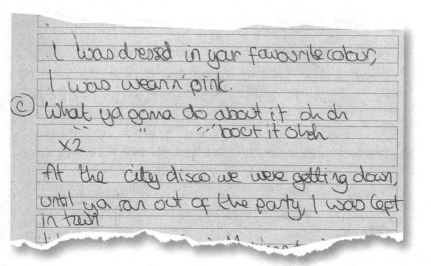

SONG

You stood me up at the cinema
What was I to think?
I was dressed in your favourite colour,
I was wearin' pink

What ya gonna do about it oh oh
What ya gonna do about it oh oh

At the city disco, we were getting down,
Until ya ran out of the party, I was left in town.
I had to get a taxi,
Maxine's taxi.

We had to have a partner in class, a girl or a boy,
You went with ya best mate Patrick so I was left with Joy.

I was waitin for a card,
Where could my Valentine's be?
I couldn't believe it when you said you'd forgotten about me.

This was written in 1994, when I was the grand age of eleven. I vividly remember 'creating' a tune in my head one day, then thinking, 'Wow, what if I put words to the tune? Then I'd have written a song!' So I did. And this was the result. Why did I bother? I have been known, aged twenty-five, to sing this to my sister on the phone – she remembers it well and it always makes her laugh.

THE CULT

HELENA BURTON

I have nothing to say about this picture, except that I am very sorry. I can't apologize enough, but I promise it won't happen again. (I can't believe they actually let me go on to do art A-level, the idiots.)

MYSTERIOUS ORA

AMANDA PERINO

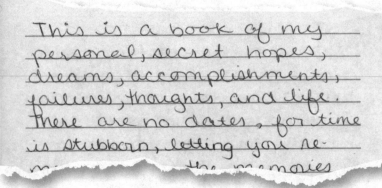

> This is a book of my personal, secret hopes, dreams, accomplishments, failures, thoughts, and life. There are no dates, for time is stubborn, letting you re-
> m... the memories

This is a book of my personal, secret hopes, dreams, accomplishments, failures, thoughts, and life. There are no dates, for time is stubborn, letting you remember only the memories in which it lets you. But I, for one, will probably be the only one to know when this small but important part of my life takes place. Know but this . . . today is January 28, 1994.

I hope you, the reader whom I may or may not know, can figure me out, for I, the writer, whom I dearly know, cannot.

Sincerely,

Amanda B. Perino '94

E I will not start off this diary describing myself or where I got this book because I already know, and I am the only one who counts or maybe even cares. Through these pages I may seem to change personalities by way of handwriting, wording, etc. Do not let this confuse you, it should actually help you understand me because that is just the way I am. To be honest, this, so far, is not the way I am. I am feeling in a wierd mood. I am feeling mysterious. I hope so far that you think I have a mysterious ora about me. Well, enough of this nonsense.

This is the first page of my diary when I was thirteen years old, followed by the first entry. I imagined myself as a veritable ocean of deep thought, but really I was just plagued by tides of hormonal mania. This was me trying to be mysterious and elusive. Did it work? You be the judge.

What really makes me die on the inside is the language that I use, such as 'for time is stubborn' or 'know but this'. I have no idea where I picked it up.

Apparently I thought that one day someone would be audience to this masterpiece, hence the references to 'you, the reader'. Destined for *Cringe* from a young age!

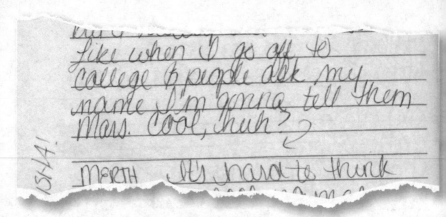

When I'm older I want a nickname. Mars is awesome. Crow is alright, but I really like Mars. Like when I go off to college & people ask my name, I'm gonna tell them Mars. Cool, huh?

> *Merth*
> *Berth*
> *Mars*
> *Crow*
> *Otik*
> *York*
> *Jupiter*
> *Venus*
> *Pluto*
> *Rylan*
> *Misha*

It's hard to think of cool names. I like Mars and York the best so far. Jupiter is alright. Venus? Maybe. Pluto is funny.

I was fourteen at the time I wrote this. I am appalled that at one point in my life I considered nicknaming myself after one of the planets. Who did I think I was – a Gladiator?

ALCOHOL & DRUGS

Caffeine, cigarettes, shandy, liqueurs, acid, spliffs, Vick's VapoRub.
Maybe not all at once.

I AM SO PRETTY

CLAIRE BATESON

I am writing this on acid, the tail-end of a trip. I need this time alone with pen and paper to express myself.

I feel really happy to be me – more gorgeous and beautiful than ever before

March 1994

I am writing this on acid, the tail-end of a trip. I need this time alone with pen and paper to express myself.

I feel really happy to be me – more gorgeous and beautiful than ever before, me in all senses. Feminine – oh so feminine – and the prettiest, most beautiful girl that ever lived. I am so pretty tonight, in the red light and the flickering of the candle. I feel separate from, and above, the other three, who all seem to be doing boring boys' things. But I am a goddess, and only James has truly seen and appreciated this. It was good flirting with the candle, playing Tubular Bells and being the only woman in the room, so desirable yet so out of reach to the others.

I feel warm and clean and sweet-smelling and radiant, I feel silken, beautiful, exquisite. We're all in my room. I have them all in my shrine, but they may not have me. Mike's taken 2 trips, I only one, but I feel above him. I feel it's my day, my trip. I feel it's my birthday.

I'm so beautiful it doesn't matter if nobody notices but me.

I can't bear reading this. I was eighteen and on my third acid trip and it made my ego expand to fill the house. Oh God. I don't do acid or ego trips any more. I'm so ashamed (more of the ego than the acid).

VOMIT

STUART BRIDGETT

> What was I thinking of? On Paper, 14ᵗʰ July 97
>
> So the end of the last thoughts left me with an attitude you could crack rocks on concerning school.
> ... after.

14 July 1997

What was I thinking of?

So the end of the last thoughts left me with an attitude you could crack rocks on concerning school. That was before. Now is, well, after. Last week up to about oh, 9.45pm on Friday was great. I was settling in nicely to the new regime. Wednesday Dave Mo Sarah Jessica + Cheeky + I went to Compton, Thursday we had a water fight at Sarah's. Friday was to be a night out at a pub.

Okay. The evening started well. I had too much to drink. My personal thoughts earlier in the day had involved a few on the fact that everyone deserves to be complimented. The only people who I didn't in fact call 'stunningly attractive' were Dave and Mo. Embarrassing, but not the worst by far. Dave asked me the question, 'Who do you fancy?'. I said, to quote, 'Well, up until two or three weeks ago I fancied Juliette Sharpe like crazy.' (True.) 'Then I went away to Loughborough and fancied Julia Middleton.' (True.) 'And I attained her.' (False.) 'Honestly, I was amazing that night. You know your counting ability is severely reduced in the early hours of the morning – I lost count of the number of orgasms she had.' (FALSER THAN A GROUCHO MARX MOUSTACHE + GLASSES DISGUISE.) Conversation slowly got started again. Uhnh. Uhg. AAAAAAAAAAAGH!

Okay – soon time to go – catch bus. Vomit. Get home. Vomit again. Go upstairs. Vomit again. (Probably embarrassment, not alcohol, induced.) Sleep. Wake up without a hangover, thank god.

Sunday – work. 8 ¾ hours of conversation with Emily. The other side of the split. I hear of Richard being upset + crying, Naomi's being upset + crying, and then Emily got upset + cried. I felt decidedly awkward. Among other things, she told me that she dreamt of me the night before and we kissed IN THE DREAM. Why did she tell me that? Hmmm? No, the you writing this doesn't know either. Very strange, and the recounts of N+R's emotions were difficult to listen to. Today, I was in shtook. Where do I sit? I sat round the corner. But at the table last lesson. My reception from the Friday night crew was unusual, to say the least. The Thoughts on these subjects could fill a good couple of rainforest acres' worth of paper + a week or two of writing.

It's the Summer Ball on Thursday and I will avoid drunkenness wherever possible. My table for the meal include all the Friday nighters, Sharon, Laura Mattson etc . . .

Watch the lady, always the lady, ladies + gentlemen. Round and round they go . . .

Where to start? I was a big anxious mess trying to coax myself into being a gregarious socialite through sheer force of will, and kept a diary to straighten things out in my mind. I would come to the 'Thoughts on Paper' folder worried and anxious, and pen these letters to a hypothetical future self, explaining everything that was going on.

I also took the opportunity to show off and try and be funny to my future self . . . which might explain why this entry seems to be written for comedic effect. I was dimly aware that social whirlwinds generally don't tend to worry about where the socially acceptable place to sit in the Sixth Form Common Room is, let alone fill pages of angstful worry on the subject, but it really did make me feel better. Contrary to these yearnings for what seemed like a better state of affairs in the social hub of my high school, I had a great group of friends, who at the time of writing had just had an earth-shattering schism. This might explain. but doesn't justify, all the dramatic references to regimes and splits, worry over where to sit . . . and so on.

The 'attained' young lady in question, who I met on a pre-university experience course at Loughborough, was a beautiful, charming girl who I literally stepped off the bus and fell for. We worked together on a project that week, staying up drinking the vast reserves of free coffee the university thoughtfully provided, and just as the whole week seemed to have accrued the required necessary narrative imperative of a really good romance story, she tactfully rebuffed my advances on the final evening, for which I had been gearing up all week.

The rest I can safely put down to inexperienced underage drinking, which fortunately didn't discourage me in the slightest.

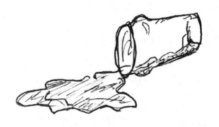

NINETEEN IS SO OLD

ALICE GREEN

> Well, it's my 19th birthday & I'm sitting here with my cup of tea and spliff listening to my birthday tape of all my favourite songs. Allan's back and I'm really glad ... ... really sweet ...

16 April 1994

Well, it's my 19th birthday & I'm sitting here with my cup of tea and spliff listening to my birthday tape of all my favourite songs. Allan's back and I'm really glad, he's being really sweet to me. So I'm pretty happy!

Nineteen, it's quite exciting! It seems so OLD when I think of what I thought of 19 year olds when I was 12. But it's still really young compared to 26 or 29! Or for that matter, 42!!

I must say I'm glad that 18 is over, it's been such a godawful year I don't want to think about it! Well I'm feeling pretty stoned so I better go. Nineteen! Wow!

Wow, how insightful! Strangely, twenty-six, twenty-nine and even forty-two don't seem that ancient any more. Then again, I was clearly on drugs . . . I've grown out of that too, by the way.

LIQUEUR SHANDIES

ANA SAMPSON

> really pissed ... ... shandys, 2 of
> which were laced with liqueur. I had one
> which was ⅓ vodka ⅔ beer. I thought
> (me Kate & Joy all did) the vodka was
> whiskey. I downed it! Then I had
> 3, maybe 4 glasses of Tennants Pilsner

7 March 1993

Went to L's last night. Got really pissed. I had 4 shandys, 2 of which were laced with liqueur. I had one which was 1/3 vodka 2/3 beer. I thought (me, Kate and Joy all did) the vodka was whiskey. I downed it! Then I had 3, maybe 4, glasses of Tennants Pilsner and some Strong Bitter and some Archers Peach Schnapps. I was utterly pissed.

Shandy? LIQUEUR!? I might have misunderstood the concept of shandy. These are just cocktails using beer as a mixer. Good specifics here – the Strong Bitter is evidently supermarket own brand. Frankly I'm surprised I wasn't being sick in the flowerbed as one of my fellow drinkers later was . . .

Chrst. My party just ended. It was a nightmare. Gordon. Phil. Coffee. Cigarettes. Smoke Alarm ba He...

19 February 1994

Christ. My party just ended. It was a nightmare. Gordon. Phil. Coffee. Cigarettes. Smoke alarm battery into freezer. Red bowl broken. 2 freezer shelves broken. Pizza wiped on the walls. Rob, Claire, Gordon, Brian off their faces. Beer and skank everywhere. 100s of empty beer bottles and cans. Broken cups. The potato. Arguing about the music. Mike dancing. It was AWFUL. Actually I thought better of some people. Never again!

This is the aftermath of the only party I was ever allowed to have (which was actually incredibly tame). What I would most like to have elaborated for me is the mysterious potato . . .

THE EAGLE FLIES BACK TO THE FOREST

ZAN MCQUADE

I didn't do any drugs when I was sixteen, but I liked to pretend I did. This manifested in me rubbing Vicks VapoRub on my temples and writing in my journal in a style I called 'trance writing', which essentially meant throwing whatever words came into my head out onto the page. Around the same time, I came across an article in *Face* magazine about travellers and the rave scene. In this particular article was a picture of a traveller named Alick blowing bubbles, naked on a hill at sunset. This, to me, was what freedom was about: being on a hill with hippies and a soapy bubble mixture. And, apparently, being painted orange.

I really feel like peeling a banana, taking a bite, and travel back to when everything was perfect. When I was happy. When I was with Alick.

His hair is still tied up, but I can't see very well. My paint shines into my eyes and they flood with saltiness. They grow tiny as they search in the darkness for his blue spots and bare shoulders. When I catch a glimpse of him, he's running fast – running away. I yell after his nudity and he slows and turns, running in a backward manner. My heart beats slow then fast, slow then fast. He is not chaste. But he looks so innocently like a man. I whisper in the darkness with my hands to my mouth, and he catches the words with his beautiful ear. Then I yell: 'J'aime les mots que tu me donne!' He laughs and runs back toward me. He takes me to the ground as marbles tumble from my pocket. I can't find them. I spit on the dog's head and we lie there, embraced, happy, tranquille. I rub my toes against his leg and he purrs contently. The tulips are still closed, the roses shut tight, the orchids haven't yet shown their plumes. But the daisy – my daisy – is full, open, laughing. He doesn't pick the daisies, but carefully observes them and respects their loveliness. Against the blue lawn their whiteness explodes and trickles down upon us with glee. We laugh and the orange sun laughs too. My hands begin to quiver as I continue to watch the dog trot cross the blue lawn to catch a frog. The river is cool. My hand runs through his hair. So soft – uniquely soft. He clenches his fist against my head and pulls me closer. His lips press to mine with no difficulty. We are interlocked for some time, as the orange sun changes quickly five times. I do not care. We are one. My gold painted body presses intently against his perfection. I cannot breath – but I don't need to. The rest of the world is as insignificant as a plum when I'm far away from the looking-glass. The pink ribbons around the bird's legs are tattered and ripped – but they are there. Oh I don't want to die I want to live where I can witness and feel and taste and love and BELOVED. I want to be loved by someone who isn't just after a part of me but after the whole thing. All of me, all of the real me.

He loves me. You don't need orange he tells me. He's right. I fold up the picnic basket and look again for my marbles. Our little game ceased to exist long ago but without pain. It was a good game – nothing like parchessi which I can't play anyway.

My fingers run up and down his arm, tracing the tea stains. I like mine with sugar – he with cream. He talks funny but I don't care. Hopefully if he decides to go away he will write me letters. That way I can spell correctly. My hand quivers more and I . . . I begin to cry. I can't figure out why the daisies wilt – then I realise. 'Je ne veux pas que tu partiras.' He looks up sharply and the eagle flies back to the forest. He comes over to me and hands me some coins and he touches my fingernail. He doesn't speak, and the banshee is silent.

(I like singing weird songs like 'Wembley' by the Candyskins. They make me feel happy and sunny and like I should be on the top of the world. If I move my head back and forth, though, something might fall out.)

GO ASK ALICE

MAUREEN LEVY

> the
> Pete Rang last nite, and asked me to
> a party at his joint. I said I'd Ring
> back. told Mum I was invited to it.
> She humed and hawed and a said
> She'd think, Well y'know what that.
> always means, She said that it might
> be a ～～～～ or something ～

23 October 1974

Pete rang last night and asked me to a party at his joint. I said I'd ring him back. told Mum I was invited to it. She humed and hawed and said she'd think, well y'know what that always means. She said that it might be a drug party or something y'know where they put dope in your drinks. THAT GOT ME THINKING! [That got me thinking I really wanted to go.]

I read a book today called 'Go Ask Alice'. It's by an anonymous girl who got hooked on drugs and it's the actual personal diary which they printed after she died, the saddest book I ever read. She got hooked on drugs at a party where there was 14 people + 10 out of the 14 bottles of coke had LSD.

I felt very depressed and confused. The girl in the book seemed so like me. It's scary!

I rang Pete and said I'd really love to come but I'd had a blow up with my parents. I was gonna go on and explain but he said, 'Yeh, I understand (as if he didn't) OK maybe some other time – bye.'

I'm so miserable.

Let's face it, I was nearly always miserable. I was an overweight, spotty kid with very little confidence and bugger-all self-esteem. I reported the non-events of my unexciting daily comings and goings religiously to the only friend who understood me – my diary.

I never heard from Pete again after this, but the author of *Go Ask Alice* became an unsavoury role model in later years . . . I don't know if I've even changed that much. I'm forty-seven, I still develop ridiculous crushes on unsuitable people and I'm still drawn to unsavoury role models . . . Hopefully when I grow up it will all be different!

MY FIRST CIGARETTE

PENELOPE MALAKETES

26 August 1991

Dear Diary,
Tonight me and Vicky my 'butt buddie' tried smoking. Well it wasn't her first time but it was mine. I kind of liked it and didn't first of all it's cool & a lot of people do it. But it kills you. I like Mike P___ a little. He's cute. I'm gonna say something like hes cute so I can go out with him I'm very eager. I need a boyfriend. Right now I hate to say it but I think I'm addicted to smoking. I'm going crazy. I need a smoke. Even though I don't inhale it I need it (sort of). My body says yes but my mind says no. One more week school starts. Can't wait!

Love,
Penni

I kept this diary between the ages of eight and eleven. The entries are mostly about which boys I like and which boys like me, but this entry highlights an important milestone in a young girl's life: trying your first cigarette. I handled it with lots of dramatic flair and reading it now I can't believe I was only eleven. It is as if some awareness, probably from films and TV, on how mature, grown-up types would act and describe things.

FRIENDS & ENEMIES

A blurry line, to be sure. Sometimes one and the same. If anything, friendship drama is a great way to hone your skills for romantic relationship drama.

POM GIRL

NATHAN GUNTER

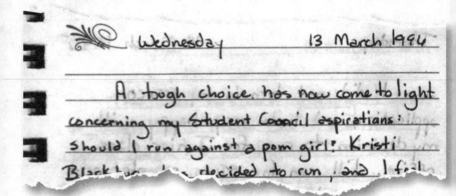

Wednesday 13 March 1996

A tough choice has come to light concerning my Student Council aspirations: should I run against a pom girl? Kristi Blackburn has decided to run, and I feel like I don't have much of a chance against her – I mean, she's a fucking POM GIRL! She's probably really popular – she's going out with Aaron Peters! What am I saying – she IS really popular! So what in the HELL am I going to do? I could run for Junior class office, Reporter maybe, but what if I'm running an impossible race there, too? I have to take the plunge some time. Not to say I don't have a chance, mind you, but I think it would be difficult. I think I will . . . maybe.

I was damned to hell if I was going to college in my home state, so starting my sophomore year of high school I became an Olympic-level resumé-padder. When I saw that there was an open seat on Student Council and no one had signed up to run, I screwed up all my courage and filled out the paperwork. I was so nervous about running, though I couldn't for the life of me tell you why now. The morning the form was due I went to turn it in and saw that a FUCKING POM GIRL had signed up; I chickened out.

I'm sure Hillary Clinton has a diary entry somewhere that is very similar to this, though possibly without the mushroom stickers.

I have to say, I find teenaged me a little cute here. I couldn't have given a shit about being popular myself, but I knew the score. As I recall, Kristi lost that race, though I don't remember to whom. I did end up on Student Council in my senior year, and I did get into that magical out-of-state college, so I'd really like to tell fifteen-year-old me not to worry so much; it all worked out okay.

PLATONIC LOVE

HELENA BURTON

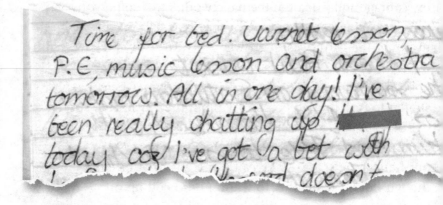

8 Jan 1991

*Time for bed. Clarinet lesson, PE, music lesson and orchestra
tomorrow. All in one day! I've been really chatting up Hoxy today coz
I've got a bet with Louisa that Hoxton doesn't fancy me. If she can get
him to admit that he does in front of me then I'll owe her a quid. If he
says no then I win. I don't really mind if she wins. I don't fancy him or
anything, but I'd say yes if he asked me out. I don't really care though,
coz he's a very close friend anyway.*

*I went to the cinema with Dan and Ben to see Arachnophobia.
When it was over I walked up Park St and got the bus home, but they
phoned Ben's mum and got a lift home. Anyway, I passed the subway
on the way home. I also passed my friend who sells the Evening Post
outside Dingles. I don't fancy him, because he's about 45 and married.
But he's a jitter and says 'hello' to me. I don't know his name, but if I
see him again I'll ask him and stop and talk to him.*

Wow, this second sentence clearly demonstrates the middle-class
upbringing that I was desperately trying to deny. Clearly, at this
age (thirteen), ringing your mum for a lift home instead of getting

the bus was the least cool thing anyone could ever do. I thought I was a wild child and very, very cool because I walked through the subway in the middle of the afternoon wearing my tie-dye leggings and Doc Martens and my mum wasn't there. This allowed me to test the boundaries of a youth gone wild and talk to newspaper-sellers in death metal T-shirts.

10 January 1991

I'm better friends with Ben and Dan now but they're always very touchy so I have to be careful (especially Dan – who is a bastard, but we like him anyway coz he's nice when he's in a good mood).

I'm a bit jealous over Hoxy at the moment coz there are loads of girls who go home on his coach with him and Ash and Milso. Half of them fancy him and he's always going on about them. I suppose he'd be going out with them if he liked them, but it makes me feel bad. The bet's still on, but Louisa hasn't done anything about it yet.

We had double biology with Mr Fuller today. I've decided he looks like Mr Desmond in the lower school and acts like Mr Park. Matt Fitcham was up to his usual perverted tricks, but I crushed him. I've found that if you push him away and look offended then he'll apologise and stop. Whereas if you get angry or upset then he just says, 'Oh you want it really' and carries on. In the end you have to beat him off and get called frigid, or let him and get called a slag. But I have found the perfect solution. Get down Matt Fitcham! I can't be too

hard on him though. He's one of my best friends, and he likes
Metallica. I've got to do my homework now, so I'll be back soon.

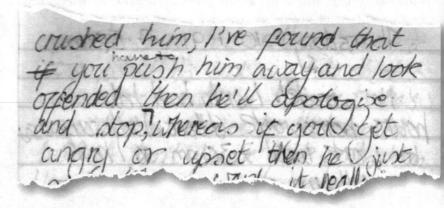

crushed him, I've found that
if you have to push him away and look
offended then he'll apologize
and stop, whereas if you get
angry or upset then he just
.... it reall....

    I don't fancy Hoxton anymore. It never does last long. Anyway,
he fancies Lisa now. He hasn't admitted it yet, but it's blatantly
obvious. Louisa and I told him to ask her out, but he said no. We
asked him why, but he wouldn't say anything. Lou wouldn't give me
the quid she owed me, though, because he hadn't actually said he
didn't fancy me, but it was blatantly obvious. I let her off coz she's
a mate.

    Dan really fancies Lou. He's invited us all to see Arachnophobia
again in the hope he can sit by her and get off with her. Not likely. She
says he's a really good mate, but she's not gonna sit by him in case he
tries it on. If she has to sit by him, she says she probably would get off
with him if he tried, but she doesn't really want to. Strange.

How did I ever manage to keep up with my rapidly changing tastes
and constructions of bizarre theories about how other people must
definitely be feeling?

    I do remember the line between frigid and slag being perilously
thin at this point in my life though. I suppose the fact that nobody
ever did anything beyond kissing and the occasionally boob-grope
made it more difficult to define.

    Perhaps seeing *Arachnophobia* many, many times helped with the raging sexual hormones. I can't think of any other reason why I would go to see it twice in four days. I suspect we spent most of the film screaming, throwing popcorn and pretending to stretch so that we could put our arm round someone, though. I can't remember much of the actual film.

Saturday 20·1·71   ... 31 PM

OOOOOOW! YAY!

I'm back from ▮▮ party (with ▮▮)
it was fucking good man. It really was
brilliant. It was the sort of party where
you didn't feel you had to be paired off
by the end of the evening, you could just
go and have fun. Well, anyway, on the
ground floor it was the kitchen (food)
and heavy metal, the next floor was
videos, above that was chart music +
... bedroom. At ...

20 April 1991

OOOOOOOW! YAY! I'm back from Jess's party (with Lou). It was fucking good man. It really was brilliant. It was the sort of party where you didn't feel you had to be paired off by the end of the evening; you could just go and have fun. Well, anyway, on the ground floor it was the kitchen (food) and heavy metal, the next floor was videos, above that was chart music and above that was Jess's bedroom.

Allie, Jess, Lozza and Kate were all a bit drunk. Well actually, most of them were faking. But Lozza was drunk coz she got ill after and was sick, but Fitcham made her drink 2 and a half pints of water after and so she was OK. Then we all went downstairs and people started arriving and the party got going. We watched the video 'Evil Dead', which scared me shitless but it was a good excuse to scream

209

and hug people. Louisa was sitting on Tom Hoskins (not bad) and after that she was lying down on the sofa with Ishmail. Ish said he felt her tits when they were both hugging each other screaming. But Louisa didn't notice, so that was OK. Anyway, it wasn't that sort of party. Although Paul and Laura were together (as always) and at certain points it looked like Jon and Jess, or Allie and Dave might hit it off. But it didn't come to anything.

The joys of young love. All punching boys in the balls, screaming and hugging. Good thing it wasn't the sort of party where everyone was expected to get off with each other, anything could have happened!

I am not sure I even knew what 'those' sorts of parties were like. I have evidence of this from when I threw a party the year before; I wanted people to get off with each other so I just locked them in a cupboard together. I was clearly more focused on efficiency than romance at this stage.

When I wrote these diaries I definitely thought they would be published rather like the Adrian Mole diaries, as a guide to being a teenager and a lesson to parents about how horrible they were to their children.

I'm rather glad that it has turned out to be just a lesson on what a twat I was. I think that's something we could all do with being reminded of now and then.

I HATE KATIE

KERRI SOHN

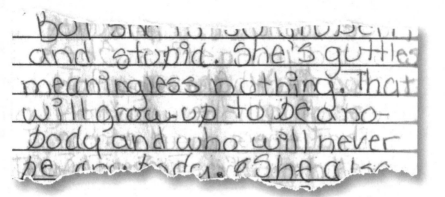

Dear Diery,

Today me and Katie got into a fight. But the problem was I didn't know what I did. Finally she said that she thinks that I always have to be better then everyone. But I don't. I think that she's just jealous of me becase I'm smarter, prettier, and more talented than her. I don't brag! I think that she just used that as a reason to dislike me. She's such a brat!!! And she's so jealous. She's also ugly and a retard! She always talks about soccer, why can't I talk about gymnastics. She's such a jerk. And worst of all she won't tell me that she's mad at me or tell me why. In front of me at least. But she has to go and tell everyone behind my back. She's a total retard!!! I think that if she'd like to say something about me she should say it in front of my face not behind my back so that she can hide behind her little stupid indiotic friends. She will probley never say that she is sorry, either will I cause I didn't do nothing. But she is so stubern and stupid. She's a guttless, meaningless nothing. That will grow up to be a nobody and who will never be anybody. She also has no spec of niceness and decence in her. She also said that all I care about is my dog and gymnastics which is not true!!!

I hate Katie Decastro
I hate Katie Decastro !!!!!
(The stupid soccer player)

I wrote this entry after getting into a big fight with my on-again, off-again middle school best friend, Katie. It was late 1993, and I was eleven. The entry makes me cringe partly because it's so mean. This girl was my best friend and I describe her in some pretty harsh absolutes. Also, we probably made up the very next day. Then there's that part where I gloat, ironically followed by a defence of 'I don't brag!' Sure you don't, little me, sure you don't.

INTELLIGENCE CHART

ALEX FRITH

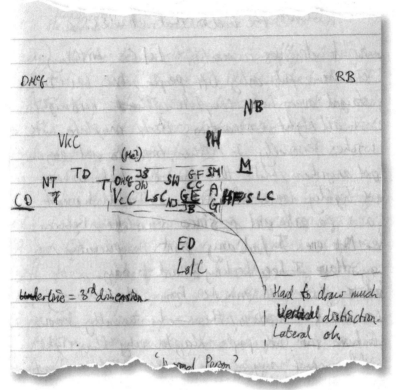

In 1996 I was eighteen and over the course of a few months I decided to work out how intelligent I thought my friends were compared to each other. This is a hateful thing to do and I'm not sure why I did it. The initials of the cleverest people are at the top, and the left-hand side is meant to represent lateral thinkers/more creative people, while the right shows people who I judged to be better at exams, knowing facts, that kind of thing. There are also some names underlined – that's supposed to be a third axis which shows people who are good with people. And yes, there's me, lurking near to, but not quite at, the very top. Wanker!

EVERY BOY FANCIES KATE

Kerry Chapple

> _...I do trust everyone alot as eres no lock on this thing. If anyone reading this – mind you're own fucking isiness. This is private._

Tuesday 31 February 1993

Spoke to DR on the phone[1] – said he couldn't come and see me this Sunday coz he has hockey trials. He wrote me a letter.

I do trust everyone alot as there's no lock on this thing. If anyone is reading this – <u>mind</u> <u>you're</u> <u>own</u> <u>fucking</u> <u>business.</u> <u>This</u> <u>is</u> <u>private</u>.

Thursday 16 March 1993

There's a rumour that Natasha says she'll have sex with 3 people at a party. God! I hope I don't lose my virginity that quick.

> _UPDATE Dee + Perky went to A1 feilds they all played spin + bottle. Kate got off with D.R_

Tuesday 23 March 1993

I got a letter from DR today. Last Sunday Kate, Mel, Dee and Perky

---

[1] A boy I had a three-week relationship with, during which I think I saw him twice and another girl kissed him.

214

went to Northfield's[2] and played spin the bottle. Kate got off with DR. I'm probably paranoid but I think every boy in Northfields fancies Kate. It's so shitty how she'll just waltz in and charm all the boys within 5 km. Why should DR fancy me? Kate's much more cocky + funny than I am and she's pretty. QED he must fancy her.

I think when I'm older I'll put my diaries in a big chest[3] to look at when I'm so decrepit that I can't remember what it was like to be 13 and 5 months. 2½ days to go till end of term. Whoopee!

23 May 1993
Nothing much, just school. Miss Barratt's decided that we're using too much loo roll and if it carries on she's going to ration it.

> I always blush, especially when I don't want to like in band etc. All of Northfeilds probably think I'm completely

28 May 1993
I've realised there is one thing I'm really terrified of is being made to look a fool. I get embarrassed so easily and always blush, especially when I don't want to, like in band etc. All of Northfeilds probably think I'm totally sad.

Oh God, these entries bring back my single-sex education with painful clarity. The angst, the pain . . . the rationing of toilet paper!? The pressure and excitement of meeting boys was, as you can see,

[2] The all-boys' boarding house across town – I went home that weekend and bitterly regretted it.
[3] Small shoebox at the back of the wardrobe, actually.

almost too much to bear. It was imperative to sign up for as many sports clubs, plays and jazz bands as possible in order to meet such boys from the twinned school across town. My acute blushing was a continual source of angst – what was worse is that I actually blushed *directionally* so that the cheek closest to the source of embarrassment (usually the first saxophone) went a deeper shade of mottled red. It was utter agony.

The entries here chart a typical 'relationship' with a boy, DR, that involved more letter-writing than anything else – it was like having a glorified pen pal. I'm not sure I ever even kissed him, but I do know that Kate, the focus of all my envy during the first few years of secondary school, got there first. She had confidence, tanned easily and, most galling of all, could flirt. I was so in awe of her I don't think I even confronted her about snogging my boyfriend.

THE PLAN AND COUSIN IVAN

NINA GOTUA

This was written shortly before my thirteenth birthday. Ana was my best friend from primary school, and when she moved away to Portugal we kept up our friendship by letter-writing. We shared the same fanciful imagination and longed to escape from our pre-adolescent doldrums to some Pacific Island paradise. (We had watched a lot of films, and had agreed that a deserted island looked very pretty indeed.) I started thinking up a list of things we'd need to take when we left, which bears witness to my passion for numbers starting with three and my tenuous relationship with logistics.

> plan to go to live on a desert
> island in Pacific. We call this ope-
> ration "PLAN". I should already start
> thinking of the things to take.
>   LIST OF THINGS FOR "PLAN".
>
>   300 kg of soap (minimum).
>   100 kg of wet tissues.
>   30 000 rolls of toilet paper.
>   300 ... ... of band aids.

17 July 1993
You know Ana and me have a plan to go live on a desert island in Pacific. We call this operation 'Plan'. I should already start thinking of the things to take.

LIST OF THINGS FOR 'PLAN'.

300 kg of soap (minimum)
100 kg of wet tissues
30 000 rolls of toilet paper
300 packages of band aids
30 000 pages of A4 paper
100 pens
250 pencils
95 bottles of sun oil
10 packs of navigation equipment
8 decks of cards
365 books
30 000 candles
300 kg of tinned meat
30 portable refrigerators
500 packs of batteries (for game boy, phone, portable radio and tv set)
5 game boys
25 games for game boy
152 games for us
2571 long and thick ropes
250 000 kg of cement
255 001 kg of bricks
5 ships
10 horses
25 dogs
11 cows
15 goats
50 sheep
60 lemon trees
105 apple trees
10 packs of strawberry seeds
20 packs of flower seeds
300 J17 (Just Seventeen) magazines

31 October 1993

Dear Cousin Ivan,

We were more like brother and sister, until you decided to spoil it all. I know you want to hurt me and that makes me madder than hell, so I both love and hate you at the same time. I have to reveal these things while writing. I want you to know, that I hate you. Yet, I will not hurt you because I still remember how we used to be so close, like brother and sister, that was until you shoved your dirty, plainlooking, ugly, stupid face into my affairs and broke the bond of brotherly love. Yes I HATE you sometimes cousin, yet I always try and start again, ignoring the truth but no, you have to look at me with your hateful eyes, which I know wish me out of your life for good. You've hurt me, damn you, you've hurt me so bad you make me want to cry, and cry so bad, I'll never stop. Our bond had never been a distant bond, but a love that a brother has for a sister. I hate you for hurting me! Never it seems can I hate you enough! One day you'll regret it, regret every time you have hurt me, only then it will be too late. I can be very mean, cousin, whatever the cost to myself. I know, you don't hate me, there is still friendship in your heart. I can use that friendship to torture you until you regret the way you've hurt me, wish you had not known me. I shall have my vengeance, you shall have your regrets. I can always die, cousin, I can always die. I shall go before you, leaving you enough time to think about the times you've hurt me. You're playing a dangerous game, toying with my heart. You throw arrows into my heart, arrows of hate, arrows to hurt me, but I can always send them back cousin, and then watch out! I'll give you a chance, thousand chances, but watch out failing all of them! I give you warning. I promise, though as I have my vengeance, I will have forgivance and give it to you, forgivance bright and soothing, for healing a broken heart.

Each time something goes good for me you have to spoil it. Whenever something goes bad you make it worser. Don't make me hate you because I don't want to hurt you, cousin. You are so hateful, so mean, yet it is not too late to seek forgivance. Remember that cousin.

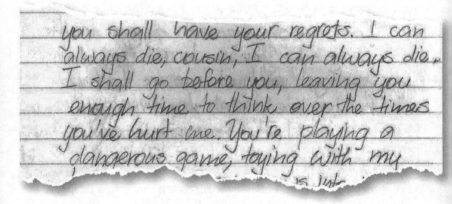

Your loving caring sister-cousin Nina

you shall have your regrets. I can always die, cousin, I can always die. I shall go before you, leaving you enough time to think over the times you've hurt me. You're playing a dangerous game, toying with my

Such wrath – this is a long hate letter to my cousin when I was fourteen. When I moved to England, he and I had to live together and share a room, which was the source of both closeness and bitter rivalry. I considered him the nemesis of my adolescence and struggled at length with my rage. I love the mix of threat and magnanimity.

The following secret note was written a day on from the previous hate letter, and it's one of my very favourite diary entries ever. It's a coded message, written in a secret alphabet:

Message: To Ivan:
Go to hell, cousin!
One day I'll have my vengeance!

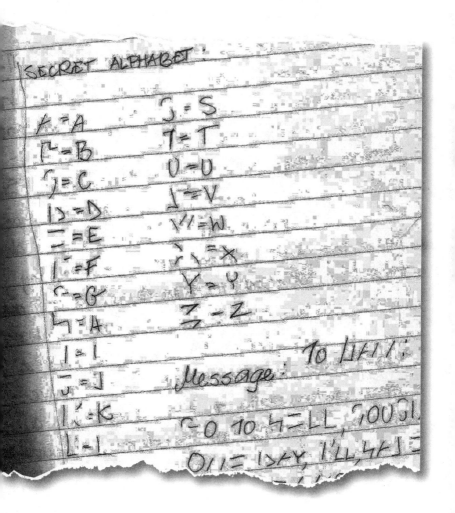

'THERE IS NOTHING
WRONG WITH TODAY'S
TEENAGER THAT
TWENTY YEARS
WON'T CURE.'

AUTHOR UNKNOWN

Also available from Michael O'Mara Books:

He Took My Kidney, Then Broke My Heart

by Dave Spikey

978-1-84317-385-4

A collection of amusing, farcical and outrageous news stories, all 100-per-cent genuine, and all framed and analysed with comic running commentary from this double British Comedy Award winner, described as 'hilarious' by Jimmy Carr.

From the man who stole a Grim Reaper costume from Morecambe Town Hall to the Leicester student who opted for suicide-bomber fancy dress – and then strolled through his city centre – no silly story is safe from Dave's laugh-out-loud lampooning. Read all about it . . .

Available now in all good bookshops and by post from:
Bookpost Ltd
PO Box 29
Douglas
Isle of Man
IM99 1BQ

Credit cards accepted
Telephone: 01624 677237
Fax: 01624 670923
Email: bookshop@enterprise.net
Internet: www.bookpost.co.uk

Free postage and packing in the UK

Also available from Michael O'Mara Books:

Tiny Acts of Rebellion: 97 Almost-Legal Ways To Stick It To The Man

by Rich Fulcher

978-1-84317-415-8

In this, the first solo book by Rich Fulcher, star of *The Mighty Boosh*, learn how to unleash the rebel that lurks inside all of us. Whether it's making rude gestures to a hotel clerk under the desk or making your own 'Do Not Disturb' sign that says 'Come In If You Like Swordplay', this book is a primer that allows us to unleash our subversive side in everyday life – without getting arrested.

Praise for the book:

'Rich C. Fulcher's prose sparkles like dew on summer corn and makes one laugh with wonder as you would at the sight of a new-born foal.'
Julian Barratt (from *The Mighty Boosh*)

'Rich Fulcher is hands down one of the funniest men on the planet and I'm not entirely sure he's from Earth.'
Simon Pegg

'Inventive, hilarious and wonderfully silly.'
Bill Bailey

Available now in all good bookshops and by post from:
Bookpost Ltd
PO Box 29
Douglas
Isle of Man
IM99 1BQ

Credit cards accepted
Telephone: 01624 677237
Fax: 01624 670923
Email: bookshop@enterprise.net
Internet: www.bookpost.co.uk

Free postage and packing in the UK